D1365363

STAR QUALITY

STAR QUALITY

THE SEVEN-POINT PROGRAM TO TURN YOUR

INNER STRENGTH INTO YOUR OUTER POWER

CHRISTEN BROWN

BALLANTINE BOOKS
NEW YORK

Copyright © 1996 by Christen Brown

All rights reserved under International and Pan-American
Copyright Conventions. Published in the United States by
Ballantine Books, a division of Random House, Inc., New York, and
simultaneously distributed in Canada by
Random House of Canada Limited, Toronto.

Grateful acknowledgment is made to the following for permission
to reprint song lyrics:

Jobete Music Co., Inc.: Excerpt from "Reach Out and Touch (Somebody's
Hand)" by Nickolas Ashford and Valerie Simpson. © 1970. Used by permission
of Jobete Music Co., Inc.

Warner Bros. Publications U.S. Inc.: Excerpt from "The Greatest Love of All"
words by Linda Creed, music by Michael Masser. © 1977 EMI Gold Horizon
Music Corp. and EMI Golden Torch Music Corp. All Rights Reserved. Used by
Permission of Warner Bros. Publications U.S. Inc., Miami, FL 33014.

Library of Congress Cataloging-in-Publication Data
Brown, Christen.
Star quality : the seven-point program to turn your inner strength
into your outer power / Christen Brown. — 1st ed.
p.   cm.
Includes index.
ISBN 0-345-38886-0
1. Self-presentation.   2. Body image.   3. Interpersonal communication.
4. Self-actualization (Psychology)   I. Title.
BF697.5.S44B76   1996
158—dc20   95-46602
CIP

Manufactured in the United States of America

First Edition: March 1996
10   9   8   7   6   5   4   3   2   1

*We have always needed stars
to show us Star Quality because we couldn't find it
within ourselves. This book is about finding and expressing
the Star Quality inside you.*

CONTENTS

ONE   Stars Are Made, Not Born   *3*

TWO   Nervousness Is Normal, So *Use* It   *25*

THREE   You Can *Tell* Your Feelings How to Feel   *59*

FOUR   You're Only as Big as You Think You Are   *117*

FIVE   Words Can Either Wound or Heal   *175*

SIX   True Power Comes from Within   *207*

SEVEN   You Deserve Star Treatment   *231*

Acknowledgments   *259*

Index   *261*

STAR QUALITY

CHAPTER ONE

STARS ARE MADE, NOT BORN

I am the greatest.
—MUHAMMAD ALI

Star Quality is power—inner "feel-good" power as well as the outer "impact-the-world" kind. When you have Star Quality, it gives you energy, vitality, and a radiance that glows from within. It frees you up to be the *star* of your life. Whether you're at a party, on a job interview, or speaking into a television camera, you shine.

Unfortunately, most people never become "stars." Somewhere along the way they stop growing. They don't work to develop their inner power or their outer presence because they don't really believe they *have* those essential traits.

Well, they're wrong. *Everyone* has the potential for Star Quality. Ken Kragen, one of the most successful personal managers in Hollywood, said it best: **"Stars are made, not born."** I don't care if it's an actor, a singer, a sports star, or a president, their Star Quality is largely due to their willingness to work on themselves and their determination to do what's needed to achieve that special niche of stardom.

Do you have to be able to fly through the air and drive a basketball to be a star? Or wear a bullet bra and sing and dance in an MTV video? Absolutely not! Described variably as charisma, personality, sex appeal, and "it," Star Quality is what makes certain people—whether a professional performer, a PTA president, a successful entrepreneur, a junior high school teacher, or a department store buyer—stand out from the norm. They may not be witty, physically beautiful, or even very bright, but Star Quality people attract us no matter what they are doing or saying. They are comfortable with themselves, and we are comfortable around them. We want to be near them. You've seen people with Star Quality—and not just on TV. Picture someone at a party whose personality is like a magnet—attracting a crowd wherever he or she stands. Imagine someone at a business meeting who, no matter the job title, commands respect. Think of people—in any situation—who put you at ease, who make you want to know them, who make you instinctively trust them. That's Star Quality.

For twenty years I've taught people how to develop their public presence, how to act on media appearances, how to speak in public, in other words, how to develop their Star Quality. During that time I've coached some of the biggest stars in sports and entertainment. Whether it's an internationally acclaimed sports star or a number one best-selling author or a beautiful movie star, I've learned that they all have one thing in common: They are all willing to do the work that is necessary to develop their own Star Quality.

There is no express elevator ride to Star Quality. You must get off on each floor and do the required work. This is good news for those of us not born with innate confidence. Those of us who don't automatically project inner strength, don't have to give up on the idea of becoming stars in our everyday life! Star Quality can be learned the same way we learn to dress properly or to handle stressful situations. How do I know? Because I'm someone who was not born with Star Quality but who wanted it so much that I've spent the greater part of my life studying it, teaching it, and breaking it down to get to its essence.

I have designed a *Seven-Point Program* that shows you how to develop your own Star Quality. Each of the chapters in this book defines a point and is filled with strategies for achieving Star Quality in your daily life. To increase your power and presence, you must *own* these Seven Points of Power.

THE SEVEN POINTS OF POWER

1. Stars are made, not born.
2. Nervousness is normal, so *use* it.
3. You can *tell* your feelings how to feel.
4. You're only as big as you think you are.
5. Words can either wound or heal.
6. True power comes from within.
7. You deserve star treatment.

Each point has several keys that will open the door to success. Here are the key messages for each point and, thus, each chapter:

1. Stars are made, not born.
- Star Quality is developed inside and outside.
- True stars *own* their power.
- Two empowering decisions you can make.
- Test your own Star Quality.

2. Nervousness is normal, so *use* it.
- Nervousness is *extra* energy.
- Make friends with fear.
- A first impression is formed in seven seconds.
- There are two keys to handling nervousness.
- Visualization is the most profound creative tool.

3. **You can *tell* your feelings how to feel.**
   - Feelings are the source of our energy.
   - Use the formulas for emotional healing.
   - The forgiveness practice is a powerful exercise.
   - Learn the rules for affirmations and self-talk.
4. **You're only as big as you think you are.**
   - Learn the Seven Points of Power.
   - Maximize your credibility by developing your physical presence.
   - Improve your voice quality.
   - Learn rapport—the key to likability.
5. **Words can either wound or heal.**
   - Learn the Six Talk Tactics.
   - Use feeling talk.
   - Power talk is speaking your truth.
   - Learn to handle tough questions.
6. **True power comes from within.**
   - Revive the Golden Rule.
   - Life is guiding you.
   - Enjoy the *here and now*.
   - Center on spiritual practices.
   - Three qualities that point to inner power.
7. **You deserve star treatment.**
   - The key to Star Quality is self-love.
   - Energy robbers and energy boosters affect your health.
   - Naturalness and humor are two characteristics of Star Quality.
   - Master the Seven Points of Star Quality.

As you can see, developing Star Quality is both an inside and an outside job. The *inner* techniques work on your core, which will strengthen you from within. They show you how to increase your mental and emotional energy so that you are able to manifest inner self-power. **All Star Quality emanates from that strong inner core.**

Once you've got inner strength and confidence, you must master the *outer* physical expression of Star Quality: You need to learn how to walk the walk and talk the talk of a strong outer expression. This book, with its various video techniques and hands-on exercises, will teach you how to develop that powerful Star Quality presence.

As your own power increases, you'll understand why true Star Quality is found just as easily in a plumber as in a president. The reason is that no matter how famous or powerful someone is, he or she is *never* better than you. Barbra Streisand put it this way: "To me, a perfect world would be a place in which we appreciate each other's differences. We're equal but not the same."

We are all unique, and each of us has something of value to contribute to the world. And once you accept that fact, all you have to do is believe in yourself—and that belief will allow you to feel equal to anyone, whether it's a movie star, a famous politician, or even an honest-to-goodness prince or princess. You'll never again have to feel "starstruck" because your Star Quality will be equal to anyone's.

You learn *techniques* to develop your inner and outer Star Quality. This is the exact process that I used to uncover my own star power. I was a flower child in the sixties when I first realized that real confidence has nothing to do with looks or brains. It has to do with essence. That realization was both a challenge and an answer to my own insecurity, fear, and pain. To find the secrets of power and presence, I first had to heal myself and become whole.

Thus, I embarked on a deep, soulful path of spiritual healing. Nothing was beyond my quest. Traditional psychotherapy, EST, Actualizations, Dianetics, yoga, meditation, Silva Mind Control hypnotherapy, biofeedback, A Course in Miracles, and the Bible were all part of my process. I spent weeks meditating in retreats, months in workshops singing and dancing my way to wholeness, opening up my heart, dealing with my shadow side, and learning to balance my energy field. I was dissolving my pain, my fear, my anger. And becoming stronger on the inside.

While my inner life unfolded, I was aware that on the outside I was still showing a lot of insecurity. I was continually smiling an "Oh, please like me" smile. I overtalked. I oversmiled. I was trying very hard to be sexy, using fake techniques such as a breathy Marilyn Monroe voice. My hands gestured aimlessly, and my head bobbed up and down, nodding like an eager-to-please dashboard doll. I knew I was trying too hard. But I didn't know what to do about it.

Strangely enough, my initial salvation was a daytime soap called *All My Children*. There was one character on the show who fascinated me—Phoebe Tyler, played by Ruth Warrick. Phoebe was a very headstrong, opinionated, powerful woman. When she spoke, people listened. That's what I wanted in a role model. Of course, she was bitchy and she was neurotic, but that didn't matter to me; I didn't concentrate on those traits. What I liked was the way she communicated directly. She got results. That was exactly what I wanted to do. So I modeled my voice and gestures after Phoebe Tyler.

I got a book and learned how to lower the pitch of my voice so I could speak in a deeper, stronger tone. I went to a voice coach to get rid of my high-pitched squeal. I used a mirror to cut down my oversmiling and taught myself to smile more appropriately.

As soon as home video cameras became available, I bought one and started refining the way I came across. I developed exercises to increase my presence. I watched actors and imitated their mannerisms. I worked on my eye contact, my gestures, and my walk until I developed a strong outer presentation. I pursued this course with a religious fervor. The driving force behind all of this was my desire to communicate with power ... with outer Star Quality. And after a while that's exactly what I was able to do.

In the late seventies, after years of working as a psychologist, I decided not to complete my doctorate in psychology but to study people directly. I'd become frustrated hearing clients speak with clarity about their problems, then repeat the same negative patterns over and over again. I wasn't interested in "shrinking" people. I wanted to *expand* them, the same way I had expanded myself.

I began working on a local television show in Los Angeles. I interviewed people on camera and began to discover firsthand the real nature of Star Quality—the very thing I had unknowingly been searching for.

The first thing I noticed was that, for almost all of the stars I was interviewing, it didn't much matter what they *looked* like; they projected a feeling of confidence because they looked good to themselves. They *liked* themselves, and because of this, we were attracted to them. Haven't you met ugly people who are sexy? Or quiet people who clearly are intelligent? Sure you have. I remember one very large woman—I would guess about 250 pounds—who had written a book about dieting. I interviewed her for a television show, and, of course, one of the first questions I asked her was, "Wait a minute, why would anyone buy a diet book from you? You're enormous." She looked me right in the eye and said, "I used to be 650 pounds. Now I am at a very comfortable weight for myself. My diet is a diet for life. I'm not interested in being a thin person. I'm interested in being happy and liking myself. I like my weight, I like the way I look, and I like the way I am."

Well, I've got to tell you—she shut me right up! All of a sudden I was interested in her book and in what she had to say. This woman had power. She liked herself; she understood her unique presence. Her Star Quality was showing!

In 1978, I founded a company called On Camera and began to teach exactly what I was learning—how to communicate with power and presence. I started doing Presence Workshops and looking at hundreds, and then thousands, of people present themselves. The initial premise was to work with people who needed to face the media or the public. That's still the main part of my business. It quickly became clear, however, that the process was a great help in *private* life as well—in developing relationships, going on job interviews, meeting people, dealing with coworkers, you name it. The people with whom I've had the opportunity to work have taught me what works, what doesn't work, and how to make personal change happen. Gradually, I developed a process that helped all my clients increase their personal power. This was accomplished by observing people directly. I began to *read* people. I watched their eyes, looked at their body language, and, most important, listened to what they *weren't* saying. One thing I learned very early on is that Star Quality is not in the words. Studies, notably one by Dr. Albert Mehrabian from UCLA, showed that words themselves are only worth about 7 percent of the value of total communication. Ralph Waldo Emerson said it best: "Who you are shouts so loud I can't hear what you're saying."

In Star Quality lingo, that translates to: The inner and the outer are one.

*Star Quality happens when your inner strength
matches your outer power and presence.*

You trust yourself. You listen to your feelings. Because you feel good within yourself, you naturally shine just like a star. Unfortunately, for most of us, this is not our experience. Many of us are playing it small. We ignore our feelings. We sneak into a room in an apologetic way. We don't love or appreciate ourselves.

I have known and worked with many "stars" of film, television, rock and roll, business, religion, sports, and politics. *They* are people who are playing it *big*, putting themselves out there; they are in love with life and all of its possibilities. On Camera is based in Los Angeles, the star capital of the world, and many of our clients are celebrities. I will be writing about celebrities throughout the book. Because of the sensitive and personal nature of our training, however, I have given our clients fictitious identities by changing their names, professions, and physical descriptions, in order to protect their confidentiality. Stars—the ones who make their living being stars—don't particularly want you to know how hard they work to appear "natural." But you will learn their secrets. You will learn how *they* learned to be stars.

Whether you are an Academy Award–winning actor or a secretary trying to impress a boss, when you are comfortable with yourself, you don't need a phony show. You don't need to put on a fake smile or try hard to be liked. You will be liked and accepted because of your relaxed, natural self.

You will see as you read this book that my work involves adjustments in both the inner and outer self. I'm interested in the root of your shyness as well as how you express that shyness. I care about what you say to yourself as well as how you present yourself to the world. And I'm more interested in how you *feel* about yourself than about how you *look*.

It's a very rare person who loves himself, who sees himself in the mirror and likes his image, who says, "I like that person. She is wonderful," or "She is strong," or "He is funny," or "What a terrific voice." I hardly ever hear that. I hear all the ways that we *don't* like ourselves. And the worst part is, I often hear it from people whom the world acknowledges as "stars"—people whom you and I try to emulate. That's why the mythological status given to "stars" is so nonsensical. We are asking these people to satisfy our projections and to fulfill our own fantasies. We put them on pedestals and admire their talent, their intelligence, or their beauty. We worship them, and they self-destruct right before our eyes. That's why it is time for each of us to get in touch with our *own* power, our own star energy. We have needed to create stars outside of ourselves only because we have been unwilling to own our power and become the stars of our own lives.

Star Quality starts with learning to accept yourself exactly as you are. From there you can make adjustments in your presence. In this book we will work on everything from shyness and nervousness to carriage, voice, gestures, and appearance. I will teach you all the inner aspects of power and presentation, just as I will show you the best way to make eye contact, how to use your gestures, how to move, stand, to connect and build rapport with people—all of the outer aspects you need to own your own Star Quality.

The outer expressions—changing your voice tone, your rate of speech, empowering gestures—can all be *easily* learned. You'll see that soon enough. The heart of this book is learning the *inner* expression of power and presence. The more we learn it, the more we feel it. The more we know it deeply about ourselves, the more our Star Quality will shine. It is the acceptance of oneself that is the true inner manifestation of Star Quality.

This quality of self-love is contagious. You like being with people who like themselves. They feel good about themselves, so you feel good about them. Even if you're jealous of such a person, that's *great*. That jealousy will motivate you to get it for yourself. That's what happened to me. The more I was around people who truly loved themselves, the more I looked at myself and said, "Wait a minute. What am I doing here? Why don't I like myself? How do they do it?"

Star Quality was something I sorely lacked. I wanted to be admired by people; I wanted to be loved; I wanted to be looked at and well thought of. It took years for me to discover that would never happen, that no one would feel that way about me until I felt that way about myself.

Each of us has our story to tell. It's easy to look at entertainment stars and imagine that they are born full of confidence. It's often shocking to learn the inside of someone's life.

Look at this man. He grew up in a physically and emotionally abusive environment.

He described his childhood as "hell."

He was a chronic bed wetter.

He was small, shy, and filled with fear.

He developed nervous facial tics.

But he never stopped working to overcome his shortcomings. He tried out for a small part in a play, got onstage, and cried and cried. He had so much to cry about, so much emotional pain, that he decided to become an actor. Rather than feel sorry for himself, he did something about it and became not only Michael Landon the actor, but a man full of confidence and, as he would say, "full of moxie."

We really do have *two* lives—the one we are given and the one we *make*. If developing Star Quality sounds too difficult for you, then let me give you some idea where I started in this process. This should eliminate any intimidation you might feel from the concept of Star Quality. What follows is an entry from my private journal of July 1968.

> I have only been married a month yet I realize I am confused and rapidly becoming more and more depressed. My entire personal life is filled with anger and depression. For the outside world, I can still "click on" and "click off."
>
> Inside, however, I am falling apart. I have no energy. Everything is an effort. Getting out of bed feels like a monumental expression of commitment to life. Death is in bed. The energy gets lower and lower until it stops. Death is a stopping. I am stopping down to a halt. Life has too much energy for me.
>
> I never think of being a star anymore. In fact, I realize I am fast on the way to becoming a dark star. I listen to someone talk to me about enjoying life, and I try, but suffering is what I know best.
>
> One day he asked me, "How can you be so unhappy in San Francisco, the most beautiful city in the world?" Didn't he know? I couldn't see the city. I didn't know the season.

The hardest work I have ever done was changing myself from an angry, hateful, fearful girl to a vulnerable, trusting, loving woman. I grew through darkness and pain, through self-hatred and self-pity, and today, in my mind and in my heart, I am a star. I love myself. I enjoy myself, and I am in touch with both my power and my presence.

The work on my outer presence happened quickly. The inner work took longer—a lot longer—but it transformed me and gave me an experience of power within myself. Each of us needs to appreciate our own unique presence. We need to know our worth.

Star Quality, I'm sure you realize, is not a static phenomenon. As you start experiencing Star Quality moments, then hours, then days, you'll find the motivation to keep building it. You'll want to spend more and more time experiencing the energy of Star Quality.

You'll start to understand that the joy of life comes when you love yourself and enjoy yourself, so much so that you become the star of your life. *That's* Star Quality.

TWO DECISIONS

Please keep in mind as you read this book that this is an educative process, not an analytical one. If the doorbell rings, you answer the door. You do not take the doorbell apart. Use this book this way. It is a simple book that will show you how to increase your power and presence by balancing both the inner and the outer aspects of Star Quality. You need to keep your attention balanced between what's going on inside of you and what's going on outside of you. You already know that to have Star Quality, your inner strength needs to match your outer power.

Star Quality is an attribute of self-appreciation. Picture the stars in the sky: They are self-luminous; their light comes from within. Star Quality people also have an inner light; they shine from within.

There are two basic decisions that lay the groundwork for Star Quality. First, make a decision:

Accept yourself as you are . . .

Say out loud, "I ACCEPT MYSELF AS I AM." Feel a little uncomfortable? That's okay. For most people, self-acceptance is a totally conditional experience; if only I were taller, smarter, funnier, tanner, you name it . . . then I would love myself. I'm always amazed at how critical we are of ourselves. At On Camera, when we tape a new client, then sit down with him or her to review the video, I frequently wince. It's like watching the short film *Bambi Meets Godzilla*. Bambi is romping in the field with flute music playing in the background. Then, Godzilla's paw enters the frame, crushes Bambi, and splats him all over the screen. This is not unlike viewing the playback at On Camera, where I frequently hear, "God, I'm fat! I'm so nervous! I need a haircut! A wig! Plastic surgery!" It's hard to believe how self-critical *everyone* is, and I'm talking about the movers and shakers: executives of Fortune 500 companies, celebrities, authors, entertainment stars.

Self-acceptance is not natural to people. What has become natural to us is self-criticism and self-judgment. Most of us have lost the ability to look gently at ourselves, to be easy with ourselves, and to enjoy ourselves. We're working so hard to be perfect and to get it right. We've lost sight of the value of our uniqueness. We've lost appreciation for what we have that is special or different from every other person we know. We've forgotten that we are a "work in progress." Because we're discontent with our imperfections and so hard on ourselves, we move into the world from a weakened place. No one else would ever be as hard on us as we are on ourselves. To give you an example of how bad it can get, I actually had a client tell me he didn't love himself because he hadn't proved himself worthy of his love. *Of his own love!*

Somewhere along the way we never gave ourselves permission to be ourselves. To be ourselves **as we are**, *without changing anything*. Nonacceptance is painful. And it's also how we try to control our world—by analyzing, criticizing, and judging ourselves and others. If you want to grow to a place where you have real control over your thoughts and feelings, you need to develop self-acceptance. Picture Mae West saying, "I never loved another person the way I love myself." Here's a woman who enjoyed being herself!

To accept yourself as you are right now, forget about being perfect and remember that yours was a human birth. Perfection is not an option. Starting here, right now, say out loud, "I AM ENOUGH JUST THE WAY I AM" and "I LIKE MYSELF RIGHT NOW. WHATEVER I'M DOING . . . I'M OKAY." You need to get to a sense of comfort with yourself. A place of all rightness. Do these statements ring true? If not, let's get to work.

Self-Acceptance

Acceptance is a very tricky thing because we've all felt unattractive, we've all felt stupid, we've all felt clumsy. This has happened to us over many years so that we have in the back of our minds a knowledge of all the mistakes we've made, of all the wrong things we've done.

It's important to heal ourselves so that we start to know that we're okay just the way we are. This book is not about taking a leap of faith and getting Star Quality. It's about doing the necessary work to develop your Star Quality.

Self-acceptance is the key. It's the parts of ourselves we *don't* want to accept, the disowned parts of us, that hold our power. Whatever we don't accept about ourselves reduces us, but seeing and accepting our imperfections is empowering because we are acknowledging the truth. Wake up and say, "You know what? It's *my* life. *This* is the body I was given. *This* is my face, my hair, my personality, my voice, my smile. I appreciate them. *These* are mine, and I'm going to accept them as much as possible, *starting right now!"*

Say you have a lot of trouble losing weight and for you it's not okay to be fat. If you're like most people, you tell yourself, "I hate how fat I am," and this is the problem—because *the things that we resist persist*. What if you accepted your weight? What if you said to yourself, "All right, I weigh 185 pounds. That may be heavy for me, but I love myself. I can accept myself at this weight. It may not be my ideal weight, but I like myself right now the way I am." This attitude frees you up to lose weight or *not* to lose weight—because, paradoxically, once you accept something, you can change it. Acceptance gives you the ability to appreciate yourself even when things are not exactly the way you would like them to be.

The second decision is simple. And, strangely enough, it goes hand in hand with self-acceptance:

You must be willing to change and to grow.

Changing and Growing

Try saying out loud, "I LOVE AND ACCEPT MYSELF. I OWN THE POWER OF STAR QUALITY. I AM A STAR." These statements are a real challenge, aren't they? If you don't *feel* like this but you'd *like to*, then you need to change and grow. Although it is simple, change is not always easy because of a condition called homeostasis. Homeostasis is a tendency toward a state of equilibrium, a condition where the motto is "Don't rock the boat. Don't make waves. Just stay afloat." Human beings, bacteria, and large organizations all have a built-in resistance to change. It doesn't even matter if the change is a good one or a bad one. We look for structure, and we are taught to fear change. Homeostasis certainly helps our bodies stay in balance and be self-regulated, but what if you *want* to change your mind, your attitude, your behavior? What if you want to expand your life? What if you've decided to go for Star Quality? Then this is a good time to realize that like nature, human beings have a natural desire to grow. Life is continuously moving, changing, evolving, growing. You've heard that the only constant is change. That's true. That's why change is not antithetical to self-acceptance. Both should be 100 percent natural so you can love who you were, who you are, and, eventually, who you will be.

But I have had clients who are determined to stay fixed. I know some very intelligent people who don't believe they can change their own attitudes. They feel, "It's too late to change the way I live" or "You can't teach an old dog new tricks." For them, this is their belief and thus it is true. Beliefs are very powerful. If you have a belief that you're not supposed to be happy, you will make yourself right even if your enjoyment of life must be sacrificed. A few months ago, a woman told me if she changed herself she wouldn't be herself: "To change is dishonest. I'm going to be true to myself. I'll never change. Take it or leave it. This is who I am."

Now these are powerful statements that, in my opinion, very few people can legitimately make. I'm sure that when we reach enlightenment there's no more need to change, but this woman had not reached that exalted level. She'd been sent to On Camera by her boss, who found her difficult to work with. Her reaction wasn't really surprising. When you're stuck, you're stuck—and boy do you dig in your heels and resist change.

In order to develop Star Quality, you must find the courage to move beyond the familiar. You need to become adaptive so you can change your attitudes easily and fluidly. Think about laboratory rats in a maze. If they run down a tunnel and there is no cheese, they will stop going down that tunnel and look for the one with the cheese. We need to be just as smart. If you're going down a tunnel with no cheese, try another tunnel. Try learning. Try changing. Try growing.

All problems are opportunities to grow. Every activity, each encounter, is a chance to learn. Change is a part of living, and if you want to improve yourself, then you need to start doing things you're not sure you can do. Each of us has the ability to change. You make a decision and you let go of what's in your way. You take risks, focus on your personal growth, and surround yourself with people who support your growth.

Make a decision.

First, decide to accept yourself as you are. Then, decide to allow yourself to change and grow.

Now you're ready to take a quiz that will assess your present level of Star Quality.

STAR QUALITY QUIZ

In the following statements, circle the answer that most closely reflects your feelings. Base your answers on your first reaction to each statement. It is important to be absolutely truthful and honest with yourself because *you are the only one who can benefit* from this quiz.

Circle one: (**T**) True (**F**) False (**O**) Occasionally

		True	False	Occasionally
1.	I may not want to do something, but if I think it's good for me I'll do it.	T	F	O
2.	When something goes wrong, I assume it must be my fault.	T	F	O
3.	I get stuck thinking the same negative thoughts over and over.	T	F	O
4.	When I am talking to someone, I worry what they may be thinking about me.	T	F	O
5.	I like most things about myself.	T	F	O
6.	I feel comfortable introducing myself to people I don't know.	T	F	O
7.	In a group of people, I am afraid just to be myself.	T	F	O
8.	I enjoy speaking in public.	T	F	O
9.	I always worry I will do the wrong thing.	T	F	O
10.	I am afraid to let people see the real me.	T	F	O
11.	My voice is an asset.	T	F	O
12.	When people look me right in the eye, I feel uncomfortable.	T	F	O
13.	I am aware of my physical appeal even if I am not looking my best.	T	F	O
14.	I tend to avoid situations in which I might feel inferior.	T	F	O
15.	I am satisfied with the way I look.	T	F	O
16.	I have lots of mood swings.	T	F	O
17.	I trust my feelings to guide me through experiences.	T	F	O
18.	I am easily angered.	T	F	O

		True	False	Occasionally
19.	My life is enriched by the people around me.	T	F	O
20.	I am a person who likes to give and receive affection.	T	F	O
21.	I speak openly about my feelings when I am angry or hurt.	T	F	O
22.	In a discussion, I have trouble expressing myself.	T	F	O
23.	I stay away from people who constantly complain.	T	F	O
24.	I am a good listener.	T	F	O
25.	I speak deliberately and forcefully.	T	F	O
26.	I have retained my sense of wonder and play.	T	F	O
27.	I avoid spending time alone.	T	F	O
28.	I trust myself to make good decisions.	T	F	O
29.	I feel I may have a special contribution to give to the world.	T	F	O
30.	I make time during the day to unstress either by meditating or relaxing quietly.	T	F	O
31.	My own self-respect is more important to me than the respect of others.	T	F	O
32.	I feel healthy, and I exercise vigorously (until I sweat) at least three times a week.	T	F	O
33.	I use humor to deal with many situations.	T	F	O
34.	I don't enjoy my work.	T	F	O
35.	I can completely let go and relax.	T	F	O

SCORING

KEY: Give yourself three points for each of the following correct answers in the answer key below. Give yourself one point for each "O" answer. As you score this quiz, you will note that each group of five questions relates to a specific chapter in *Star Qual-*

ity. If you score low in any of these areas, please spend extra time reading and working with the related chapter.

Questions 1–5 = *Ch. 1 Attitude*
Questions 6–10 = *Ch. 2 Nervousness*
Questions 16–20 = *Ch. 3 Feelings*
Questions 11–15 = *Ch. 4 Outer Expression*
Questions 21–25 = *Ch. 5 Talk*
Questions 26–30 = *Ch. 6 Inner Power*
Questions 31–35 = *Ch. 7 Energy*

ANSWERS	POINTS	ANSWERS	POINTS
1. **T**		21. **T**	
2. **F**		22. **F**	
3. **F**		23. **T**	
4. **F**		24. **T**	
5. **T**		25. **T**	
6. **T**		26. **T**	
7. **F**		27. **F**	
8. **T**		28. **T**	
9. **F**		29. **T**	
10. **F**		30. **T**	
11. **T**		31. **T**	
12. **F**		32. **T**	
13. **T**		33. **T**	
14. **F**		34. **F**	
15. **T**		35. **T**	
16. **F**			
17. **T**			
18. **F**			
19. **T**			
20. **T**		TOTAL SCORE	

IF YOUR SCORE IS:

95–105: You've got a good jump on Star Quality with your positive attitude and high self-esteem.

84–94: You're above average, but if you want to develop your Star Quality, you've got some work to do.

73–83: You can really benefit by working on your Star Quality. See in which areas you score lowest, and do the exercises that accompany these chapters.

0–72: We've got work to do! Let's get started!

CHAPTER TWO

NERVOUSNESS

IS NORMAL,

SO *USE* IT

I go through life working with two basic emotions:
fear and suppressed fear.
—COMEDIAN DANA GOULD

Dana's got it right. That's what we're handling. When people tell you they get up in front of groups and never feel any anxiety or nervousness, don't believe them (unless, of course, they're on drugs). Feeling nervous before you get in front of people is normal behavior!

Actress Ellen Barkin told Liz Smith that she felt nervous backstage at the Oscars, but discovering that Paul Newman and Clint Eastwood were also nervous made her even more fearful. After all, she figured, "If *they* are nervous, then you know *you* should fall apart."

People come to On Camera all the time to get rid of their nervousness. I always say to them, "Nervousness is just *extra* energy. Why would you want to get *rid* of energy?" And that's the point:

Nervousness is extra energy.

You *can learn* to use your nervousness and get it to work for you. As someone once said, "You don't want to eliminate the butterflies—you just want them to fly in formation."

Nervousness is a self-perpetuating act. When you're nervous, you think you're drawing unwanted attention to yourself—which makes you *more* nervous. It's a vicious cycle, but there are studies that show the quivering, perspiring, and fidgeting you're going through when you're nervous is often overlooked by those *not* having such uncomfortable sensations. Similar studies show that even when observed by friends, highly anxious people were judged to be no more anxious than a low-anxiety group. That's because when you're nervous you feel that all eyes are fixed on you . . . but the truth is that the person most aware of your jitters is you.

Sometimes it's hard to distinguish when someone else is nervous, but it's easy to know when *you're* nervous. Hands shake, voices get tight, we forget things. This all happens in normal communication, so it's only natural that it happens in front of groups. But groups don't really notice an individual's fears. Honest. I always tell my clients: "If you want to make sure people know you're nervous, you have to either pass out or throw up. That way you'll be sure to make your point."

Now you say, "My hands *really* shake." Okay. Most people's hands do some shaking, especially when appearing in public. If I held mine out right now, you would see some trembling. The difference is, I consider this normal. I'm not going to let myself get upset about it. If I get in front of an audience and I get a frog in my throat, I clear my throat. If I forget where my train of thought is going, I pause and come back to that thought *when I'm able* or move on to my next thought.

You see, I don't resist nervousness. I let it move *through* me. It's absolutely normal to make mistakes. It's not a tragedy. Mispronouncing words is normal. Everyone does it. Scratching yourself in public is normal. So is having your voice crack. Perspiring is normal. Feeling your heart pound before a presentation is 100 percent normal.

Let's go back to somewhere between the ages of six and nine. You had to stand up in front of the class and speak about something you brought to school. Remember show-and-tell? Compositions and book reports came later and were much easier. All you had to do was read what you had written. Show-and-tell was sort of scary. You had to talk extemporaneously, and you had to look at the class as you spoke.

For most of us, public speaking stopped there. Future politicians went on to the debate team, and thespians joined the drama club. The rest of us avoided the spotlight. That avoidance got even easier in college. The professors were doing all the presenting. All we had to do was stay awake and take notes.

Out in the real world at last, pursuing our careers, we discovered to our horror that show-and-tell skills *are* required. People were fighting for center stage. In the marketplace, competition demands that everyone be a salesperson. And the first rule of salesmanship is *You must sell yourself!* Appearing in public or before the media provides fantastic opportunities to "strut your stuff and do self-selling."

The first time I spoke to a large audience, I was thirteen years old. The teacher/sponsor for the gymnastics club insisted I was the only person who could talk to the student body about this club. This was a terrifying idea since my junior high had about eight hundred students. I walked onstage, approached the podium, and said, "Mr. . . ." into the mike. The sound was deafening. My voice rang all over the gymnasium. Everybody was talking, so I paused and started again. "Mr. . . . Mr. Peters." I managed to get out another sentence or two, and then I flew off the stage. Who had prepared me for such a horrifying experience? Why would anyone want to hear her voice blasting through a public-address system? I was shaking all the way back to my seat, which was up at the top row of bleachers. When I reached the second-to-the-top row, my foot slipped and I managed to fall through the bleachers. This was a feat I had not conceived was humanly possible. I was always skinny, but to slip through the bleachers? Only everyone else's laughter helped me see the outrageous quality of this moment. I was physically unharmed, so I would have to say that I survived my first public speaking engagement. I also learned to fear public speaking.

That's the amazing thing about the brain. It learns so quickly and so well. That was a tremendous learning achievement for me: Every time I saw a podium, I remembered to feel terrified.

FEAR OF SPEAKING

The Book of Lists by David Wallechinsky and Irving Wallace identifies speechmaking as the number one fear of Americans, ranked right up there ahead of fear of flying and fear of death. *People are more afraid of giving a public speech than they are of dying!*

I was once adjusting my clothing backstage getting ready to give a talk to the sales representatives for Princess Cruises, and I pulled on a loose thread at the bottom of my skirt. It was a nylon thread and functioned like a rip cord. Seconds later, the hem dropped completely out of my skirt. I walked onstage with hemming tape hanging from five inches of unraveled hem. I said, "Sure the bottom just dropped out of my skirt, but not of what I came here to tell you . . ." You talk about these things. They make you human and draw the audience to you.

"*I feel I will make a fool of myself in public.*" This belief was shared by someone who had never so much as tripped in front of an audience. And, believe me, I have had clients who have literally fallen down right in front of the podium. One woman forgot to take off her cordless mike, used the restroom, and returned to her seat to a standing ovation. Another man was on the dais at USC, and when he stood up to speak, someone in the front signaled him that his fly was open. He hastily sat down and zipped the tablecloth into his fly. The next time he stood up and walked toward the podium, he cleared the table. Dishes flew, glasses smashed onto the floor—and this man can laugh about the situation.

Even sales has its hazards. People cough, choke, and stutter when they ask for money. Their eyes dart, their voices tighten, and their palms sweat. Appearing on television can be equally frightening. I have had clients who, before I worked with them, walked onto a talk-show set, backed up to sit down, and missed the chair completely. Others emitted loud burps into the microphone due to an acute case of nerves.

What we're dealing with here is simple fear . . . fear that can be managed when you face it directly. I see it every day in my work. A client comes in. We chat for a while. Then he or she goes in front of the camera to speak, sell, or be interviewed. The fear of exposure is enormous. And I've discovered after twenty years of coaching that it all comes down to their fear of just being themselves.

If we criticize, judge, or berate ourselves, we weaken ourselves. And from a weakened place, it's difficult to get in front of a camera or a large group of people or even *one* person and feel comfortable.

Managing Fear

Here is a story about how one of our clients, a well-known record producer, learned to handle his fear. Rod had a palpable fear of appearing in public. He arrived twenty minutes late, jangling with tension. "I'm so sorry! My office is right around the corner, but I had a meeting in Encino with Mariah Carey and the freeway was jammed!" Rod is a transplanted New Yorker—aggressive, intense, five o'clock shadow, Afro hair. He gets right down to business.

"I don't want to waste our time here. I've agreed to appear on *Nightline* the night before the Grammy Awards ceremony. Ordinarily, I don't give interviews. I don't need the publicity. But I like this guy Koppel, so I agreed to be on his show. They're shooting Tuesday night at my house. I'm going to be sitting in my den with ten million people watching. I'm starting to freak!"

It took me half an hour to get him calm enough to go before the camera. There were no hidden issues, only successes to trumpet, but Rod's fear was so palpable even I was getting shaky.

That's because:

Anxiety is a communicable disease.

We ushered him into our closed-circuit television studio and onto our talk-show set. The camera operator started to videotape the first interview. It felt stilted. Although he answered all my questions dutifully, the mood was joyless. The room felt airless; my stomach tightened. We watched the agonizing playback together. On screen, he was tilted to one side, his hands locked against any gesture, stumbling over his words, licking his lips, his eyes wandering, color pale. Halfway through, he stopped me. "I can't watch this. That's not me up there. I can lecture to hundreds of people with no problem. But on camera, I'm a mess!"

"You're too worried about what you're saying," I told him. "People want to get to know you. Just like you're at home in your den, you should be relaxed, feeling good, telling stories. Instead, you look like you're about to face the firing squad. Your face is full of fear."

Rod told me he was self-conscious about his hair. "I guess I'm used to being behind the scenes, hiding out."

I asked him about his childhood. I'm not a therapist, but sometimes the key to unreasonable fear lies there. "My mother hated to have her picture taken. I guess I caught the terror. I never posed for a picture in my life. All I've got is snapshots, snapshots, snapshots."

"Your hair is not the problem," I told him. "Get it trimmed and shave just before the show, you'll look fine. Wear a blue shirt and a jacket and you won't need a tie."

He laughs. "You picked up that I hate ties, right? That's why I chose this crazy business—so I can look like a slob." He is beginning to loosen up. I want to get him back up on camera.

I introduce a visualization exercise. "Close your eyes and take a moment to breathe. Imagine yourself seated in your den, facing the bright lights, cameras about to roll. You feel the rush of excess energy you used to call nervousness. This time, instead of throwing you, it fills you with confidence. You're a very successful man. You are about to share with us some of the energy and optimism that typify you. It's fun to talk about your work."

"Okay. What've I got to lose? If it's not me and it's terrible, I'll really be pissed off. If I'm me and it's terrible, at least they can say, 'Hey, this guy's terrible! I can be successful 'cause I'm better than this guy!' That's all right with me."

The next time in front of the camera, Rod was much more relaxed. He freed up his hands. His face came alive. He started to talk about the record business, the people he had worked with, the lessons he had learned. As we watched the playback, Rod got excited.

"My face is relaxed there. I look like I'm happy to be here, to be part of the party! I've never watched myself and been happy—ever!"

The transformation was remarkable. "How come my face can look so different this time than the other?" he asked.

"You've learned to use the extra energy you used to call fear. **Because you've managed your fear, you're able to move freely in the present moment.** You've dropped your resistance to being seen."

As a "mock" interviewer, I asked him on camera, "Do you ever get scared . . . scared that the magic will go away?"

"I'm scared all the time," he answered. "What I do is take the fear, and, instead of being paralyzed by it, I catalyze myself with it. I make it work for me. I create a vision—a result I want to achieve—and use the fear as one of the components to fuel it."

"That's great," I told him. "Koppel will love that. You're talking from experience. We *feel* it as well as hear it. That's you up there."

"I felt good. I was on. I knew where I was going." He dropped his voice but not his intensity. "Before, I could never watch myself because I imagined a horrible result and projected it."

Like many quick studies, Rod was soon reciting a little mantra, a litany of "do's": "Breathe—enjoy the extra energy—make eye contact—forget about how this will look—enjoy the moment, stay present."

As he shook my hand at the door, he laughed. "You know, I should know all this stuff. The people I work with, the stars, they're monsters of energy. It's the energy, not the information, that most people get. I went to therapy for nine years; I spend two hours with you and I'm all right."

You can see from Rod's story that if you simply use your "extra energy," it's possible to change fear into something that works for you.

HANDLING NERVOUSNESS ON THE OUTSIDE AND THE INSIDE

The benefits of getting comfortable when you're in front of people are enormous. You don't have to switch personalities, change your voice, or act like someone you don't know every time you speak in public. You can be yourself and develop your own natural style. You also don't need to announce to your audience, "I'm nervous. My knees are knocking." When you do that, you're just reinforcing your own fear and making the audience think they have to worry about you too.

The physical symptoms of nervousness, like sweaty palms, dry mouth, shortness of breath, and butterflies in the stomach, are not nearly as important as how we *interpret* these symptoms. When you understand that nervousness is normal and that nervousness produces extra energy, then you start to see your physical reactions as a positive sign that you are emotionally ready to speak in public.

Changing Personalities

Most of my clients start out interpreting these physical symptoms as fear. To justify this fear, they need something to be afraid of. So they begin to imagine what could happen to them:

> "I'll be embarrassed . . ."
> "I'll make a complete fool of myself . . ."
> "I'm going to bore them to death . . ."
> "I'll die."

It gets pretty dramatic. The mind creates extraordinary reasons to justify the fear. One client told me she imagines she's giving a performance and all these critics are sitting in the audience criticizing her looks, her gestures, her words, everything she does. In order to combat this, she stiffens up. She becomes formal and changes personalities, hoping this artificial behavior will somehow be better than the way she usually talks. It never is.

You already know that before you speak in public, you're supposed to get nervous. Your heart rate should jump a few minutes before you begin to speak and again when you first start. Use this surge of extra energy to animate your talk and give it life. Your nervousness won't last long; it will begin to drop off within about thirty seconds.

One-on-One Conversation

Acting, performance anxiety, stage fright—all involve *performing* for an audience. Leave that to the professionals, please. When you make a speech, what you want to do is *communicate*. Think of your speech as normal everyday conversation. The only difference is you spend a lot more time organizing the content.

When an executive comes to On Camera with a prepared speech, we immediately put him on camera and tape him reading the speech. After a few minutes, I stop the tape and say, "Forget about giving a speech. Just talk spontaneously to me. Put the speech in your own words, using your outline as a guide." No longer is he worried about performing. He's having a one-on-one conversation with me. He's learned an important point:

You can only speak to one person at a time.

He is no longer trying to *perform* for an audience but is using his own natural gestures, inflections, and facial expressions to communicate.

Next, we rewind the tape and show it back to him. Mr. Peepers comes alive. He is speaking *to* the audience and not *at* them. Forget performing. *He's communicating.* Think about Ronald Reagan, who has been called "the great communicator." He never *delivered* a speech. He talked one-on-one in an intimate manner.

Talking privately (one-on-one communication) is an important concept, one I have used with people who are required to speak to as many as 10,000 people at a time. Rather than have them spinning around trying to speak to all of those 10,000, we teach them to speak to one person at a time. That they can do. The other 9,999 people can watch.

Facing Fear

Your thoughts create action. Have you ever been getting ready to give a talk to a group of people and said to yourself, "Oh, I'm going to blow it!" If the answer is yes, then you probably *have* blown it. We scare ourselves. We feed the fear. We disconnect. A good example is when you're speaking and you feel yourself "just talking." You feel loose and disconnected from what you're saying. People have even told me they consider public speaking an out-of-body experience. That's fear. It contracts you. It separates you and causes you to feel that you are losing yourself. So on the surface, it would seem that fear is something to be avoided. *Not at all.* **Fear is a fact of life—and it can't be avoided.** It can, however, be controlled. It can be understood. And it can be used. Actor Kelsey Grammer has an interesting way of controlling his performance anxiety. When he speaks to large audiences, he keeps his car keys in his back pocket. It calms him down, just knowing that at any time he could just get into his car and drive off.

Fear is a natural, normal part of life. You are going to experience it whenever you take risks, explore new territory, meet challenges—whenever you grow. After all, *what you grow through is your fear.* In fact, if you move away from fear, you move toward a helpless place where you're stuck, immobile. The idea is to look for fear. To move *toward fear* so that you can expand and grow.

The more successful you are at handling fear,
the more successful you will be in your life.

You continue to grow through fear—the fear doesn't just go away. All that happens is you become stronger and develop trust in your ability to handle new situations. And as you take more risks and move through your fear, you begin to realize that you can handle *anything* that comes your way. That's what's so interesting about fear. It deepens you. Knowing that you can face the unknown gives you power.

Around 1975, I had an opportunity to face my fear of being on television. I was volunteering at a small cable television station when a producer asked me if I wanted to try interviewing an author on camera. I was terrified—but I agreed. My hands were shaking, my stomach tightened, but I looked into the camera and introduced myself and my guest. Several minutes into this half-hour show, I relaxed enough to have a spontaneous conversation with the author. The conversation seemed to be very lively. My fear diminished until I heard him say, "That's the dumbest question I ever heard." I don't remember what I asked him, but I remember my fear returned—and quick! I remember thinking, "If I have to go, God, I'll go now." But, of course, I didn't die. One doesn't actually die of embarrassment. I managed to complete the interview and move through the fear. It was a difficult experience, but I faced it. I survived the unknown, and I was free of one more fear. As a bonus, I found I actually enjoyed being on camera.

Because we are so used to fighting our fear, trying to move away from it and avoid it, I have designed a couple of exercises to help you appreciate and learn to *use* your fear. Obviously, we're talking about fears that block your growth and expansion—not fears that protect your health and safety.

When do you use these exercises? Let's say you are meeting a new person and you feel afraid. Or you're changing jobs and you feel some queasiness. This is when you must embrace the fear, not run from it. Tom Cruise told *Vanity Fair*, "I've always had this thing that when I was afraid, I never backed off. I always went forward." Do this, move into your fear. Take action. It's pointing the way for you to grow. It's the first rung on the ladder reaching toward Star Quality.

EMBRACING FEAR EXERCISE

The first time you start to feel the fear, whether it's a queasiness in your lower abdomen, sweaty palms, or shaky
legs, say:

"Yes! Thank you. I am taking a risk. I am meeting a challenge. I am becoming stronger."

Feel the fear. Move through it. Let it be your ally and point
the way to your growth.

This exercise works for simple, nonparalyzing fear. But what if
you feel totally blocked? What if the fear is taking over your body?
Now it's time to release it. Get that feeling *out* of your body. Stuck
energy drains you. You've got to *move*. The next exercise is one I
do when I'm feeling that being a human being is too hard, when
I feel trapped, afraid, when I have forgotten that I have a right to
make an ass out of myself.

Unless I achieve enlightenment in this life—which looks doubt-
ful—I accept the fact that I will have fear. And you must accept
it too. So use it, ride it, make friends with it. It's your teacher. Believe it or not, you can release it and enjoy letting it go.

RELEASING FEAR EXERCISE

Stand up. Take five really deep breaths. Breathe in and exhale loudly through your mouth. Start making sounds while you exhale—moaning sounds, angry sounds, animal sounds. Whatever is comfortable for you. Push yourself. Get wild. Scream, yell, shout, stamp, get that fear unstuck. Be totally unreasonable. Let the fear move through you. Get it out of your body. Cry, laugh, release.

Frustration

Frustration, like fear, needs to be handled internally. We create our own frustration by our reaction to events. Long before I knew how to handle frustration, I used to unleash it in frightening ways. I remember when I was in San Francisco, quite a few years ago, I was having a particularly bad day. While parking the car in an underground garage, I got way too close to a large concrete pillar. I pulled the car forward and backed into the pillar on the driver's side. It would have been normal simply to pull forward and make a correction. But no, I was too frustrated and upset. I just kept backing up, configuring the car around the pillar. By the time I cleared it, the entire side of my car had been bashed in. Thousands of dollars' worth of damage taught me a lot about frustration control. When celebrities "lose it," it makes the news. Comedians had a ball when Jack Nicholson stopped at a traffic light, took a golf club out of his trunk, and proceeded to bash in the windshield of a man who had cut him off in traffic. For weeks, the buzz was that he must have been out of his mind to use a three iron; a wood would have worked much better.

It makes much more sense to scream inside your car on a highway or to pound a pillow to release the emotion. You learn to *ride* your frustration just like you ride your fear. I remember an On Camera session at which one of our clients, a successful actress, brought in a Hi-8 minirecorder. She also brought her director, who was shooting the session for her with the same camera she had used to film some home movies on location for the film she was currently making—and, unfortunately, her director forgot to change the tape. As a result, he taped over all her wonderful memories. She went white; sparks flew out of her eyes. This was irreplaceable footage. No one knew what to do. She excused herself, went to the bathroom, and five minutes later entered the room ready to work. She was a pro and knew how to move past her frustration and back into the present moment.

Someone said that the key to life is getting massive doses of frustration. The better you are at handling it, the more successful you will be in *all* situations. Think of it. Once you can handle frustration and rejection, what can stop you?

Shyness

Celebrities experience shyness just as easily as anyone else. Sally Field has described herself as having a "crippling shyness." This from a two-time Oscar-winning actress who has been in the public eye for three decades.

Shyness is not difficult to understand: *It's a fear of being yourself.* If you're afraid that being yourself won't be enough, you start to withdraw. You wonder if you have other people's approval. You contract yourself, and thus you're considered shy.

I'll tell you a story to show you how this works. We were coaching a very high-profile athlete. His name was all over the sports pages; his contract was mucho millions, and his managers were very concerned about the way he came across when he met people. He was shy.

The first time I met Charlie, what impressed me most was the placid expression on his face. When he was introduced to me, he stuck out his hand, looked down at the floor, and kept his face blank. His palm was enormous, but it wasn't so much that I was lost in his hand. It was that his hand didn't talk to me; I squeezed, and he didn't squeeze back. I would have said it was like holding a dead fish, except his hand totally enveloped mine, so the dead fish was holding me.

His eyes did not rise to meet mine until several seconds into our greeting and only then with darting, fleeting glances. It was clear why he was visiting On Camera. After all, we form our impressions about each other in the first seven seconds after we meet, and first impressions are generally the most lasting.

For the first five minutes, I did all the talking in order to remove any fears Charlie might have about what was going to happen. Then, I took him to our talk-show set and our videographer taped our interview. He recorded an opening greeting so Charlie could see exactly how he was coming across. I shook his hand, only this time I just laid my hand in his—pretty much fingertips only—and gave him the experience of someone who was unwilling to make contact. We talked for several minutes on camera. I asked him some silly questions and kidded him a bit, just to make sure that the camera would pick up his smile.

When Charlie saw himself on camera, he was quite surprised at how little eye contact he was really making. He saw his eyes darting and shifting around; he realized he was making it difficult for the two of us to make contact. I explained that the eyes are the most expressive part of the body—they are the first place you establish contact.

When he saw the effect of my handshake, I could look at him and say, "Get a grip!" He understood that you have to get your palm into the other person's palm and *squeeze* if you want to give a real handshake.

We went back to the videotape to see his heartfelt smile. It was big; it was infectious. It was clear that this smile could warm a room, and he saw this as strongly as I did. This time I said, "I'd like to introduce myself, Charlie." I stuck my small hand in his large one; we both squeezed while making eye contact and smiling. Now my impression of this guy was very positive. By the time Charlie left the studio, he was giving me the touchy-feely high five and low five, but he also had a good classic handshake. So what do they mean "You never get a second chance to make a first impression?"

Worrying

If you have a strong fear of failure, chances are you're very good at worrying. I was at a party one time where they had hired astrologers to entertain the guests. A woman asked for my day and time of birth, did quick calculations, and said I was a natural warrior. I thanked her, and she gave me a strange look. I said, "I feel very strong, and I think it's great that you see me as a natural warrior." She paused and said, "I said you were a natural *worrier*." This was a horse of a different color.

Right then and there, I decided to get a handle on this worry thing. I read a study that showed that habitual worriers, even if they could solve all their problems, would *still* find something to worry about. I realized that I needed to develop a way to handle worry.

The technique that works best for me is to pick a specific time and place for worrying. I have a room and a chair that I use for my worrying, and I like to schedule "worry time" either early in the morning or at midday. In this way I can happily stew about anything from the night before as well as anything new that comes up during the day that I might not have had a chance to fret about. I retreat to my room and worry as much as I can about everything I can think of. I wear those worries out. Then, as soon as I get tired of worrying, I'm off to do something more interesting.

If worries come up at other times, I know exactly how to handle them. The other night I woke up at 4:00 A.M. with a little voice rattling in my ear. It was telling me I had made too quick an edit cut on a videotape I had been editing that day. I started reviewing the tape in my mind, making corrections. I even started worrying about how I was going to correct it. Then I said to myself, "*Stop!* You have a place and a time to worry. This is the middle of the night. This is something I will think about tomorrow in my worry chair." Then, I went back to sleep.

THE TWO KEYS TO HANDLING NERVOUSNESS

Through my work at On Camera, I have learned to handle the symptoms of my nervousness. I now know that nervousness is normal and that by channeling my energy and using my fear, I can let my "nerves" work for me.

Sound easy? Well, it is—if you master the two powerful keys that let you handle nervousness:

1. Relaxation
2. Visualization and Imagining

Once I learned to relax myself and visualize what I wanted to happen, speaking in public became not just easy but enjoyable. I suddenly had control and finally understood why they had to give some people the hook to get them off a stage. It's *fun* speaking in public. Your energy rushes, and you feel high. You don't want to stop. This infusion of energy becomes seductive and compelling.

Sound like something you'd like to experience? Start by learning the first key—how to relax yourself. Then move on to the second key and train your mind to visualize your success.

Relaxation

Anxiety used to be a normal part of our survival mechanism. You're probably aware that in ancient times, the anxiety response of "fight or flight" could save your life. If there is genuine danger, an anxiety response produces extra amounts of energy and oxygen . . . and you're out of there. If you're facing an audience, however, fleeing should not be your first choice. What you want to do is relax yourself. Relaxation is the body's natural antidote to anxiety. You cannot be anxious and relaxed at the same time. All you have to do is relax yourself and the anxiety leaves. I have a three-step process to handle nervousness:

1. First, release your muscle tension.
2. Second, breathe from your diaphragm.
3. And third, practice rhythmic breathing.

These three steps will help you handle *any* physical symptoms of nervousness.

The first step to relaxation is to tense the appropriate muscle, then release it. Anytime you want to let go of tension, you just tighten your muscles, then let go and relax. This is the fastest, simplest, and best muscle destressor I have ever found.

Whenever you are sitting down somewhere just waiting—it can be in your car, at the office, or on the phone—mentally scan your body for tension. You'll recognize the signs—tight shoulders, a stiff neck, muscles that hurt when you touch them. When you find tension, contract and tense these muscles even more. Inhale, hold, and contract. Exhale, and let those muscles go limp. Feel the tension leaving you.

TENSE AND RELEASE YOUR MUSCLES EXERCISE

Stand, sit, or lie down. Get comfortable. You are going to start with low tension, then progress to medium and high tension. Inhale and tighten consecutively your feet, calves, thighs, buttocks, abdomen, stomach, arms, chest, neck, and head. When the inhalation is complete, your entire body should be tensed. Hold to a slow count of three. Exhale and relax all your body parts, starting from the head down. Relax completely. Feel the stress draining from your body.

Now for the second and third steps to relaxation . . . proper breathing.

Relaxed Breathing

You don't have to be a singer or an athlete to learn how to breathe correctly. Relaxed breathing is a pulse-calmer, mind-regulator, and tranquilizer. Slowing down your breath and exhaling longer than you inhale calms the mind. The breath needs to be deep, even, and regular. It's *deep* inhalations that help remove nervous, distressing feelings.

Smooth and continuous breath flow
relaxes and calms the nervous system.

It's easy to understand why slowing down your breath and inhaling deeply reduces anxiety. Breathing is a process of inhalation and exhalation, of expansion and contraction. If you inhale and

---

DIAPHRAGMATIC BREATHING EXERCISE

If you are a chest breather, let's take the opportunity right now to shift to abdominal-diaphragmatic breathing.

Lie faceup on the floor. Place one hand on your chest and one on your stomach. As you breathe in, your stomach should move while your chest remains still. When this happens, you know you're breathing correctly. Practice breathing the same way while sitting and then while standing. Put your hand on your abdomen. It should rise and fall like a balloon filling and emptying with air.

---

exhale rapidly, very soon you will be gasping for breath—and mimicking a state of anxiety. You hear this right before someone introduces him or herself: "Hi ... (gasp) ... I'm Sue."

Your breathing reveals your state of mind. When a person is breathing rapidly, you can always see the tension. So it figures if you learn to control your breath, then you can relax and calm your mind. Some of us breathe so well, taking slow, deep abdominal breaths, that we completely relax ourselves *just* by breathing. Others cut off their breath, keep it shallow, and gasp, instilling tension as they breathe. The rhythm and rate of your breathing actually helps create your mental and emotional state.

So how do you get to a place of deep breathing? By using your diaphragm. As you inhale, your abdomen should rise, and as you exhale, your abdomen should fall. Then, chest breathing is replaced by deep, even, and steady diaphragmatic breathing. If you breathe into your abdomen, you can take in up to ten times the air as a chest-only breath. Unfortunately, the average person uses his chest muscles rather than his diaphragm when he breathes,

RHYTHMIC BREATHING EXERCISE

Practice extending your breath by sipping air in slowly through your nostrils; double the count as you let the air out slowly through your mouth. In for three, out for six to start. As you get comfortable, increase your breath rhythm to in for four, out for eight; then in for five, out for ten. Relax your jaw. Notice your diaphragm expand. Breathe out slowly, and feel your diaphragm contract. Continue to do this rhythmic breathing for a minimum of three minutes when you want to slow down and relax. This is what I do to relax myself before a public presentation.

and this breathing is often shallow and rapid. The lungs don't get the air they need, and, as a result, anxiety is produced.

Try looking down. If your belly expands when you breathe in, you are breathing from your diaphragm. If your belly doesn't move, you're breathing from your chest only.

Breathing deeply from the abdomen gets more oxygen in our blood. In natural childbirth, it's called the cleansing breath. Take a few deep breaths, and now let's learn to relax ourselves by lengthening or extending our breath. Rhythmic breathing just blows tension away.

Feeling a surge of nervous energy before a presentation or an important meeting or a first date is an experience nearly everyone shares. My feeling is, if you're nervous—great! We know you won't be flat. The challenge is to let that energy work *for* you, not *against* you. Most of our clients appear in public. This is the exercise we use to show them how to get their energy to work for them:

CHANNELING YOUR ENERGY EXERCISE

• *Start with a simple stretch.* Stand and stretch your whole body upward. Inhale, and raise your arms up over your head. Exhale forward and down, letting your upper body go completely limp. Hold and breathe, feeling the stretch increasing with every exhalation.

• *Slow down your breath.* Use your rhythmic breathing technique. In for four, out for eight. In for five, out for ten. The deep breaths will oxygenate your blood and help you feel calmer.

• *Shake out your arms and hands.* You don't need to lock your hands or bob your head. Don't let your hands fold together or your arms cross at your chest. Let your gestures complement your words. Use this extra energy to animate your gestures.

• *Smile with your lips and your eyes.* That way, you begin your presentations with a bright look. Breathe through your lips and vibrate them. Stretch out your mouth. Let it relax.

• *When standing, plant your feet so that your weight is evenly distributed.* This way you won't sway. Shift your weight first to one side, then the other. Next, plant your feet in the center. Feel a sense of balance. If you're seated, get balanced while sitting forward in your chair.

That's all you need to do to get that extra energy to work for you.

Visualization and Imagining

The second key to handling nervousness and getting yourself in the right frame of mind is learning to use the power of your imagination. Visualization is the most powerful method we have for training ourselves.

You're breathing diaphragmatically. You've relaxed the different muscle groups in your body. Now you're ready to do something you do every day: You create a mental picture, then construct your life from this plan. Sounds good, doesn't it? You create an image of whatever you want to achieve and then go out and do it. That's exactly what successful people do. They imagine what they want, see it in their mind's eye, and then they create it in their life.

All success begins with the imagination.

Arnold Schwarzenegger credits his success with being able to visualize what he's wanted and then creating it in his reality. All the way back as a boy in Austria, he visualized himself as a bodybuilder who would become Mr. World and Mr. Universe. From there he imagined himself becoming one of Hollywood's hottest stars (when nobody else could), and the rest, as they say, is history.

We don't all visualize the same way. Some people visualize by seeing clear Technicolor images, while others just get a vague sense of what they're creating. Some people even use their sense of hearing to imagine with. The truth is that visualization can take place through one or any combination of the five senses. The mind and the emotions create reality. When you're just sitting around thinking about something, you're projecting ahead in your imagination. You're imagining the future.

Fear Fantasies

Visualization is a very powerful tool. Unfortunately, many of us use it to disempower ourselves. If you visualize yourself as a clumsy person who trips in public and always says the wrong thing, you have a very good chance of creating this in reality. Remember that your brain is like a computer: It believes what you program into it. It has no way of knowing if the good messages or the bad messages are true. It simply acts on the information that is fed into it. Therefore, you must *program* your mind to do what you want it to do. *The subconscious mind does not know the difference between imagined and real.*

If you're using this powerful tool, your imagination, to create Fear Fantasies, then you could be living out some real horror stories in your life. Some people let their Fear Fantasies power their life. They imagine not having money, losing their boyfriend or girlfriend, getting sick. And they use the power of their imagination to create a negative reality. This is the imagination run amok. If you want to have inner power, inner strength, and success, then you must use your imagination correctly. You must get it to work for you. You can use imagination to plan out your future.

Success begins with intentional imagining.

Mental Rehearsal

If you have a powerful-enough image of yourself doing something, that something gets recorded by your brain as though you've actually done it. There is a study in which a group of skiers were hooked up to machines that measured muscle tension and when they imagined themselves skiing down a mountain the muscle tension was exactly the same as when they were actually skiing. In another study, basketball players used visualization exercises to improve athletic performance. One group visualized themselves shooting baskets, then went onto the court to play. The other group did no visualization, just went on the court and played. The group that consistently made the most baskets was the group that visualized beforehand.

If athletes can use this technique to improve their performance, why can't we use these same techniques to improve our lives? By going through this process in your head, by doing a mental rehearsal, you are setting the stage for a success. You are learning to visualize yourself as you could be rather than as you are.

KEYS TO THE POWER OF IMAGINATION

- *Relax yourself.*
- *Start with something small.* For example: If you're afraid to mingle and socialize at parties, picture yourself walking up to a stranger. Hear yourself asking him if he likes the music. See and hear his reaction and envision your response.
- *Create a clear visual image.* See, hear, and feel what you want to create at the party.
- *Employ as many senses as possible.* What would you be doing with your hands? What would you look like? Sound like? Feel like? Let yourself feel the power of your imagination. Create a success for yourself.

I've seen visualization techniques work wonders for people. One client, a successful television personality, wrote a book about the joy of being with a man. She was single at the time I coached her. But she told me without reservation that she knew as soon as she finished her book, she would find her man. "I see this happening quite clearly," she told me. "He is tall, attractive, loving—he even has money," she gushed.

She was attending a cocktail party to celebrate the publication of her book, and WHAM—there he was. She called to tell me, "I've met my man. He is everything I knew he would be. I'd been seeing him for months inside my head." It's been five years, and they're still happily married, cavorting around the world celebrating life—another testament to the power of the imagination.

What follows are visualization exercises that you can use to increase your comfort in social situations, at informal buisness meetings, when giving a public presentation, or when being interviewed. They work for all moments when you need to present yourself—on a date, in a business meeting, at a party. The techniques and the results are the same. It makes no difference if you're speaking to Congress or to your PTA or if you're going to a party or a business meeting—you do these exercises to establish a comfort zone. Above all, remember: All successes begin with the imagination.

VISUALIZATION EXERCISE: FOR SOCIAL SETTINGS

This visualization exercise should be used to get yourself in the right frame of mind to attend a party or other social function. First, you need to read through the instructions. Then make an audiotape of yourself repeating the following text with feeling. After you've made this tape, take a hot bath or shower. Feel the hot water relaxing you. See your problems being washed away. Feel the excitement of going to see old friends and meeting new people. When you finish getting ready, look in the mirror and see that you look attractive. Now sit down, put on this tape, and listen to yourself saying the following words:

• I am breathing rhythmically and relaxing myself. I feel safe.

• I see myself walking into a party, smiling as I introduce myself to several people. I enjoy meeting new people and finding out about them.

• As I interact with other people, I am pleased to notice my own ease. I realize that I feel this way because I appreciate myself and enjoy sharing who I am with others.

• Knowing that I create my own joy, I relax and enjoy the evening. I feel fulfilled because I am comfortable with myself and others.

VISUALIZATION EXERCISE: FOR INFORMAL BUSINESS MEETINGS

To prepare yourself for a business meeting, you need to start first by reviewing some of your successes and reflecting on your abilities.

Support yourself by taking deep rhythmic breaths from the diaphragm, breathing in your feelings of power and confidence, breathing out any tightness or stress you may feel.

Read through this text once. Make an audiotape of yourself saying the following words. Speak slowly and distinctly. Play this tape back and get the feeling these words bring.

• I enter the room, make eye contact, smile, and shake the hand of each person I meet.
• As I speak I express myself clearly and concisely. I remain aware of my talents and abilities. I communicate my message with power and presence.

Use this exercise to put you in the right frame of mind to express yourself confidently in any business situation.

VISUALIZATION EXERCISE: FOR PUBLIC PRESENTATIONS

First, read through this exercise. Then make an audiotape of yourself carefully speaking the following words. You may need to tailor them to your needs. Close your eyes and play this tape back. Allow yourself to experience this visualization exercise fully.

• I am sitting in my chair waiting to be introduced, feeling confident, relaxed, and energized. What I once called nervousness, I now know is just extra energy available to me to empower and enhance my presentation.
• I am introduced. As the audience gives me a warm welcome, I confidently approach the lectern. I pause, survey the audience, smile, and feel happy to be there, knowing I will represent myself and my company at our best.
• I take a deep, relaxed breath, establishing eye contact with one person in the audience, and begin to feel I am communicating with each person in the room.
• In my desire to share this significant information with everyone in the auditorium, I project a strong and positive presence, and each person in the audience is impacted by my powerful presentation.
• I deliver my speech with ease and confidence, sharing my enthusiasm about my material in an energetic manner. As I complete my talk, I receive a rousing applause from the audience, which is acknowledging me and the excellent job I have done. I thank them and walk confidently back to my seat feeling very satisfied and content.

VISUALIZATION EXERCISE: FOR INTERVIEW SITUATIONS

Make an audiotape of yourself speaking the following words. You may need to tailor the language slightly to fit your situation (I've chosen a job interview). Close your eyes, and play this tape back. Allow yourself to experience this visualization exercise fully.

• I am sitting in a chair, waiting to be introduced to my potential employer. I feel confident, relaxed, and energized. What I once called nervousness, I now know is just extra energy available to empower and enhance my personal presentation.

• I take a few deep rhythmic breaths from my diaphragm with extended inhalations and exhalations. As we introduce ourselves, I smile and feel happy to be here, knowing I will represent myself at my best. I establish eye contact with the interviewer and whoever else is present and begin to talk with confidence and ease.

• In my desire to share my information with all the people in the room, I project a strong and positive presence and imagine I am reaching each person individually.

• I proceed through the interview relaxed and confident, sharing my enthusiasm about myself, my knowledge, and my abilities in an energetic manner. When the interview is complete, I feel a sense of satisfaction for a job well done.

CHAPTER THREE

YOU CAN *TELL* YOUR FEELINGS HOW TO FEEL

The purpose of childhood is to get us so screwed up that we have something to work on as adults.

— ANONYMOUS

Feelings are the source of our energy. If we wall up and cut ourselves off from our feelings we may feel no pain, but we will feel no joy, no satisfaction, no excitement either. To feel really alive, we have to give up our fear of being hurt and let ourselves truly experience all our feelings. It's by letting ourselves feel on the deepest levels that we are able to heal our fear and sadness. We release the energy that holds these feelings in place. As we unlock our pain and communicate our feelings openly, we are able to express freely who we are. We begin to display our essence—to express our inner Star Quality.

One of our clients, Gwendolyn, said to me, "Feeling good has replaced looking good as my goal." I couldn't agree more. To feel good, thoughts must flow freely through our minds and feelings flow freely through our bodies. When our thoughts or feelings get stuck, we block the free flow of energy. This causes us to feel a whole slew of negative feelings—anger and depression being chief among them.

Tell your feelings how to feel is just a clever way of saying that you can have control over your feelings. You don't get control over them by ignoring them or pushing them down. You get control by *feeling* them. You then begin to value your feelings and what they are saying to you. As your emotions flow through you, you learn not to indulge yourself in them but to experience them, sometimes limit them, and many times redirect them. It's natural to experience negative emotions like anger or fear; the goal is not to get *stuck* in them. When your emotions are out of control, it's as if you're living on a roller coaster. You feel ugly, so you must *be* ugly. You feel stupid, so you must *be* stupid. You feel nobody loves you, so you must be unlovable. You are what you feel.

Healthy self-discipline creates emotional balance in one's life. You achieve a balance between feeling your feelings and telling your feelings how to feel.

When you started working with this book, we mentioned two decisions necessary in order to develop Star Quality. One was **a willingness to accept yourself as you are**—and the second was **to allow yourself to change and to grow**. There is a third decision that needs to be made if you want to develop a strong emotional basis for your own Star Quality. Decide to **give yourself permission to feel all your feelings**. To do this, you must know that *you are stronger than your fear*.

ADDICTIONS

Addictive behavior results when people block their emotions and don't express their feelings, then use their addiction to *avoid* feeling. Alcohol, drugs, food—they all serve as poor substitutes for feeling.

I had one client who had a serious addiction that got in the way of the work we were supposed to do together. She's an older Hollywood star, a real grande dame.

She had written her memoirs and needed to be coached for her interviews on the talk-show circuit. She was a fascinating woman with lots of stories to tell, but she was not focused and was resistant to my coaching. She said to her assistant, toward the end of the first hour, "I'm going to need a whole new wardrobe for this tour."

Her assistant looked at her and said, "Don't be silly, Anne. You just *bought* a new wardrobe. You have your new Chanel suits and your favorite Valentinos in several colors. You have hundreds of things in your closet that would be perfect for this tour and would look fabulous on camera."

Anne turned to me and said, "I'm going to need an entire new wardrobe for this tour, am I not?"

Now I looked at her, and because I had heard the stories about her, I replied, "Am I talking to Anne the sane rational person, or am I talking to Anne the compulsive shopaholic?"

She lowered her head as she replied, "The shopaholic."

I said, "Then you're going to need an entire new wardrobe. I would suggest that you get on the phone right now and call your dresser and make an appointment as soon as possible to choose the outfits you will need for this tour."

She excitedly shouted to her assistant, "Get Phyllis on the phone!" Then she said, "We'll need to go to Neiman's. I'm not sure I've seen everything they have in the designer collections. Make a call to Armani's representative. I'd like to go through their suits one more time."

We both knew we were dealing with an addiction and that she wasn't going to solve her addiction in my office that day. Shopping was her drug of choice. This is what she used to avoid the pain. Each of us has to make a choice either to heal the pain or to try and avoid it through addictive behavior. At this point, Anne did not have the strength to heal her addiction. It takes great courage to do what Betty Ford did when she got help for her alcohol addiction and then went public with her story. Anne's "solution" was short-term, but it enabled her to do the work she had to do—and from that point on, she did it well.

MY EMOTIONAL HEALING

As one of my well-known clients said to me, "I don't have any physical pain, all my pain is emotional." That's what we're healing. It's not surprising that so many entertainment stars are in therapy, working to let go of the emotional pain.

It took tremendous courage for me to push through my self-pity, anger, and fear. Of everything I've done in my life, I consider my emotional healing to be my biggest accomplishment.

As a child, whether I was late to the dinner table or forgot to do my math homework, I didn't feel that I had *made* a mistake, I felt I *was* a mistake. I began to believe all the negative words that were hurled at me. I was bad, stupid, selfish. It didn't seem to matter whether my father was screaming at me or whether my mother wasn't speaking to me. Whatever happened I blamed myself. It was I who caused their anger and their pain. The guilt was enormous.

After I left home at age twenty-four, I was still miserable. I eventually realized that I was treating myself the same way my parents had treated me. I was continually telling myself how stupid and selfish I was. The horror of all this wasn't just that I was treating myself badly and screaming at myself the way I had been screamed at for so many years; I was out in the world screaming at strangers, parking-lot attendants, employees, friends. Hate, guilt, and anger were inside me, and I projected my feelings onto the world. My inside and my outside matched.

I hated myself. It got so bad I even thought about the release of death. I had lots of pills and was seriously thinking of taking them. Death held a real attraction for me.

At that point, I had a choice. I could take the pills and die or I could find a way to live. As much as I was attracted to death, I realized I hadn't really *tried* life. I was aware that some people were indeed *enjoying* life. They were staring at sunsets instead of dark apartment walls. They were listening to music instead of hateful voices inside their heads. I had no interest in sunsets or music, but I did have a curiosity about a happy life. I decided I wanted help.

A Paid Friend

Not knowing where to go for help, I got out the Yellow Pages and looked up psychologists and social workers. After talking to three people, I settled on a strong and kind woman—a social worker named Ellen.

I was candid with her. I did not have any close friends. I was in great pain and was more attracted to death than life. I was miserable. Could I pay her to be my friend? Could she show me how to like myself? She asked me to write a letter in my journal telling my parents how I felt.

The letter I wrote was filled with anger. In fact, my anger was only exceeded by my pain. I knew how to blame, so I blamed my parents for my self-hate. I blamed them for my insecurity. I blamed them for my fear. I was a victim, and it was all their fault.

Ellen encouraged me to get into my anger. Apparently, it was good for me to feel anger toward them. Better that, as she pointed out, than turning it inward against myself. My huge depression—my desire not to go on living—had been caused by turning my anger inward against myself.

My Rage

I wanted to talk to her about my parents and the things that had happened in my family, but I liked to do it with distance. I could look back, but I didn't want to go back there emotionally and experience my feelings. She kept asking questions and prodding me, but this didn't have any effect on my deep-rooted anger, which just seemed to have overtaken me. My heart would race, my stomach would tighten, and then I would attack. I had been attacking strangers, men I dated, and friends for a long time, but it never seemed to make me feel better. In fact, it made me feel worse. I would feel depressed and irritable after an angry eruption. So it made no sense for me to go back and get upset about the past. I didn't want to reexperience that particular anger.

Ellen and I continued to see each other. I regaled her with my stories, always devoid of emotion, and she talked to me about healing my past, about dealing with my emotions. It took months of talking before I trusted her enough to work on my pain.

One day, I had talked enough. I was mad. I used my fists and I pounded those pillows. The anger, the rage flew out of me. I had so much hate for the way my father had treated me. "You bastard!" I yelled. "I hate you." Pounding, screaming, swearing until my anger dissolved into shaking and my rage turned into tears. I felt so sorry for myself, so sorry for the way I had been treated, so sad for myself. I sobbed and sobbed. I was wallowing in self-pity, but at least I was no longer showing this phony happy mask to the world. The sweetness act was gone. I was sad, and I was mad.

About this time, my parents came to California to visit me. I went to their hotel to see them. I said to my father, "I am a mess. I don't like myself, and it goes right back to my childhood. I blame you, and I blame Mother. I understand that you did the best you could do as parents, but that doesn't do anything for me or my self-hate. I need help. I need therapy, and I hold you both responsible."

"I'm sorry you feel this way, Chris," he responded. "I wish there were something I could do!"

"There is," I replied. "You can take out your checkbook and write me a check that will begin to pay for my therapy."

Watching my father write this check was some sort of a validation. Inside I knew that his father had screamed the same abusive words at him that he had screamed at me. It went back to my father's father and his father before him. He had paid the price, and I had paid the price—*in pain*. Only in his day you did not go to get help. In my day you did.

My goal was to let the feelings rise in me, to let me feel all of my feelings without getting stuck in them. I had been bent out of shape for a long time, holding on to my angry, sad feelings—almost out of habit it seemed. I had hidden them and kept them locked inside me.

My Victimhood

As I released my pain, I looked for ways to manage my emotions. I had a lot of practice being a victim and had fallen into the habit of blaming others for everything I could. "I can't believe he did this to me" was a normal justification for one of my upsets. It took me a long time to realize that people don't just *do* things to you. I had a choice whether or not I let those things happen. Only *I* could make me upset, not some other person. What freedom I felt when I started to take responsibility for what happened to me. It was exhilarating. I stopped looking at things from the point of view of "Why me?" and started to realize "Why *not* me?" I was not being victimized. I was living life. Life has problems, and I finally began to know how to deal with them—by accepting my own responsibility for them.

The secret is:

*You are the only person who can get yourself upset
or let something happen to you.*

I had learned a bad pattern and had gotten myself into the habit of being a victim. Once I started being responsible for my feelings, I felt a whole lot better. I developed a strong sense that I could control my own life. This knowledge gave me power. I was starting to understand what a friend meant when she said, "It's never too late to have a good childhood."

My Wrath

Dealing with and learning to handle anger was tough. Something seemed to be wired wrong inside me. When someone would ignore me or raise a voice in irritation, I would become furious. It was almost as if I felt my very life was at stake. People were threatening me, and I felt I had only one choice—attack.

Like so many women, the place where I was really messed up was with men. I was in therapy letting the anger fly at my father, but even as I was recovering from that abuse, I was abusive to the men I dated. I was insulting and would try to pick fights.

I could only date angry men. They were the only ones who attracted me. In my rage I would sometimes push men or throw food at them, counting on them not to retaliate. But I never thought I would find a man who was a perfect emotional match for my rage. I did.

Jim was a successful and manipulative man who liked to scream and yell. He would create scenes in car washes and restaurants. For him, sparring and fighting were like food. I couldn't yell at him enough.

It worked for me. Here was an attractive, successful man who liked to be yelled at. He wasn't Daddy, but he would do.

I got to scream out my anger, stand up for myself, and find my voice. I acted out my rage until I got sick of the yelling, sick of the fighting, and sick of hearing my own voice.

The nice thing about this episode was that I no longer felt the need to attack people. I had been angry and overbearing to the max. Now I noticed that my aggression was mellowing into assertion. I used to walk around feeling that I didn't count. Now I was able to agree or disagree with people and express myself without always feeling that someone was deliberately out to harm me. I was developing boundaries, and I found that I used my anger a lot less. It was no longer the way I defined myself. People could say or do things that bothered me, but more and more I would stay detached. Another person's behavior no longer affected my feeling of personal self-worth.

Healing Anger and Sadness

Sometimes I find we need to wail, howl, scream, and get our feelings out. I no longer keep my emotions locked inside, but I also don't recklessly push them onto people either. I have a healthy respect for my anger; I also consider it dangerous to other people. Therefore, I have two rules:

RULES FOR ANGER

1. Don't store it inside you. Express it in the privacy of your room, car, closet, garage. Let out the shouts, jump up and down, scream, hit pillows or a punching bag in a contained environment.

2. Stay away from people until you've either released your anger through loud lamentations or you've taken a cooling-off walk.

Having been abused with senseless anger, and having abused others with my own, I know the value of disengaging from people during the first few seconds of anger. While practicing deep breathing, I take a cooling-off walk around the block. This tends to disperse the anger and bring me back to balance.

Each of us needs to learn to handle anger, whether it's our own or someone else's. Handling our own anger may be more difficult than handling someone else's. When we are angry, we've already taken something personally. We've plugged in emotionally and need to take steps to unplug ourselves. It's easier to stay detached when someone else is angry at us.

CUSTOMER SERVICE

Good customer service people are trained to stay calm and detached even when someone is screaming at them.

Lydia was always considered to be a marvel among her fellow telephone company customer service representatives. She was known for being able to handle even the most hardened cases. Her technique was easy:

"I just move back and I keep moving back. I give them lots of space to express themselves. If they are screaming, I move the receiver away from my ear, and let them rail on. When they're done, I tell them, 'It's okay with me if you're angry. I can take it. I've been married.' Even if they don't laugh, at least they know their anger didn't affect me. At this point, we can go to work on solving their problem."

Lydia understood she didn't need to teach people to better handle their anger. She just needed to get out of anger's way so she could do her job. For some people, this is not so easy.

SHORT FUSE

Bob was a hotshot salesperson for a huge manufacturing company, and he'd just told his boss where to put it. The company's human resources manager called me with a giant dilemma: "We have a lot of money invested in this guy. He's a big producer. But he has a horrible temper and attacked his boss in front of several people. His boss wants to fire him. We will fire him but would prefer to keep him if he'll change. Can you help?"

Bob sashayed into my office. He was very good-looking in a rugged, athletic sort of way. A strong voice and a ready smile added to his confident demeanor. He knew why he had been sent to see us but acted as if he were here for an office social. After a few minutes of small talk, I introduced him to one of our trainers, who would also be working with him, and asked, "Is what the human resources manager told me true? Did you tell your boss where to put it?" This was all it took. I might as well have waved a red flag in front of him. His tone was loud and irritated when he replied, "It was totally justified. You don't know the whole story. Listen to what the guy did to me."

I said, "You're really angry with me."

"Yes," he replied. "You're trying to make me wrong."

"It doesn't feel good, does it?" I asked. "This is how it works, Bob. It doesn't work to attack people and make them wrong."

He answered boisterously, "He *was* wrong. He's not going to mess with me. I sell four times as many products as anyone in our division."

"So that gives you license to tell your boss where to go? You're so valuable to your company, you can treat anyone you like with a total lack of respect?" I asked.

He glared at me as he answered, "No."

"Let's go into our studio and act out this scenario," I said.

Our trainer played the boss, and Bob played himself. He told us the story. It seems that Bob expected his boss to give a party for one of the guys who had been promoted and was leaving for Chicago. But his boss didn't have the budget for any kind of farewell party. Bob was outraged. By the end of this role play, he was yelling at our trainer (his boss).

"I counted on you. You are a total ass. You let all of us down. No one can trust you," Bob said.

The trainer replied, "Then why do you make this event all my responsibility? If you wanted it done, why didn't you organize it and do it yourself?"

Bob was in the pattern of trying to get others to do things, and if they didn't do them, or didn't do them to his liking, he would make the others wrong. He needed to understand that he had a choice in how things would turn out.

We explained to him that you only have a few seconds after an event occurs to get yourself under control. Each of us, at the moment when deep anger rises up from within, needs to learn to take several deep, calming breaths or get up and go for a cooling-off walk. If you decide simply to go with the anger and rev your body up, the cost can be tremendous. If you haven't been able to release the anger, then don't communicate with anyone until you have.

The cost of his anger was enormous; his job was on the line. We asked him, "What are your long-term goals?" Amazingly, Bob wanted to become the manager of his division. As I pointed out to him, "In order to manage a division of people, you first need to learn to manage yourself."

SADNESS AND FORGIVENESS

Anger is a generally destructive emotion that needs to be carefully managed. Interestingly, when anger is allowed to take its natural course, it is often a precursor to tears and sadness. Usually, when I let my own anger out, I see that right underneath it is sadness. In fact, if I let myself feel all of my feelings, I can often skip the anger and go right to the sadness and vulnerability.

It's natural for us to cry when we're sad, yet our culture restricts an open display of emotion. We're often thought of as weak if we cry or display our emotions in public. So we choke back our feelings and become hardened in the process. We keep our emotions under tight control, and the cleansing release of tears is denied us. Tears contain water but, most important, stress hormones that are released by the brain during periods of intense emotion. Cybill

Shepherd has said that learning to cry kept her sane during the tough times in her life. That's because crying is natural. It is healing. It helps wash away the pain.

Through experiencing sadness, I gradually became aware that I did not know how to accept myself. I felt lonely and unloved. I was very hard on myself, but I didn't want to be. I wanted to learn to accept and to forgive myself.

One of my clients had written a book on forgiveness. As I read his book in preparation for his coaching session, I was struck by the power of forgiveness to heal oneself. This is what I *hadn't* done; I hadn't forgiven myself. I was still carrying with me all the things I hadn't forgiven. No wonder I felt so burdened and so sad.

As I thought about forgiveness, it seemed like a big job. I was overwhelmed when I realized how much I had to forgive myself. All the areas in which I didn't accept myself—where I was still judging and criticizing myself—would have to be healed.

What a concept. I was a person who felt I always had to be tough, to keep the pressure on, to push myself if I were to succeed in life. Now I was imagining what it would be like to forgive myself, to find the ease and trust that come from self-acceptance. What would it be like to stop all the pushing and just "be"? What if I were able to bring all these dark stuck areas to the light to be healed? If I forgave myself, would I let go of the pain of the past? Did I *want* to let go? After all, when something is forgiven, isn't it forgotten?

The answer, of course, is that to forgive oneself is the most liberating, joyful experience in life. It is not forgetting—it is facing the truth and understanding it.

The Forgiveness Practice

To this day, with all the healing work I have done on myself, I find the forgiveness practice the most powerful tool I know to gain self-acceptance. Because I am willing to do this practice over and over and stay with it through the pain and the sadness, I have learned that I can gently open to forgiveness, but I cannot push myself into it. It may take time until I'm ready to let go. I just stay with it—however long it takes. It *will* happen because the heart knows how to forgive.

THE FORGIVENESS PRACTICE

Write these phrases once a day, seventy times, seven days in a row. Use your own words to describe what it is you want to forgive yourself for. Start by writing:

I, (your name), forgive myself completely.
I, (your name), forgive myself completely.
I, (your name), forgive myself completely.

Keep going. When things come up for you, include them. For example:

I, (your name), forgive myself completely. I hate my impatience, but I forgive myself for it.
I, (your name), forgive myself completely. I can't stand my thighs, but I forgive myself for them.
I, (your name), forgive myself completely.

Keep writing, let go and feel the release, the freedom that forgiveness brings.

The process of forgiveness goes on and on. It doesn't stop. It's sometimes very painful. It's always very freeing. What it does is lighten you up. It gives you an experience of self-acceptance and self-love, which in my mind is the best feeling there is.

Don't be surprised if tears flow—the process is that powerful. If you just stay with it, writing, "I, (your name), forgive myself completely" seventy times for seven days in a row, you will find unknown things for which you need to be forgiven. You'll find that you may resist this process, but if you have a strong desire to heal yourself, your resistance will soften. This practice allowed me to forgive myself for my cystic acne, for having a father who screamed all the time, for feeling afraid, for doing whatever I had done. I just forgave myself for being human.

In the beginning of my forgiveness practice, I was focused on other people and what they had done to me. I was reveling in my victimization, blaming as many people as I could for my life. It took me a while before I could let go of what others had done to me and just accept what had happened as my own doing. I finally realized that whatever happened happened to *me*—and it needs to be forgiven *by* me.

In order to use the forgiveness practice, you need to look at the areas where you don't forgive yourself. The destructive, angry, hateful, mean, judgmental parts of you all need to be forgiven. Just start this practice and let the unhealed areas surface. When you are willing to face whatever is in you, you can truly accept yourself. Remember the first condition: self-acceptance. You forgive yourself and learn to accept yourself as you are. After you accept yourself, you can make changes. Forgiveness and acceptance come first.

If I wonder whether I am complete with my forgiveness practice, I use this simple check:

ACCEPTANCE EXERCISE

Start writing: *I accept myself as I am.*

Write this twelve times. Then go to a mirror and while looking directly into your eyes say, "I accept myself as I am."

If your forgiveness work is complete for that moment in your life, you will feel loving and accepting of yourself. If you disagree with this acceptance statement and are unable to accept yourself as you are, go back to the forgiveness practice and continue writing. You may want to adjust your writing to thirty-three times a day for seven days in a row.

Self-Forgiveness

Recently, a tall, elegantly dressed man walked into my studio with the demeanor of a naughty boy. Since I first coached him eight years ago, he had become nationally recognized as a motivational expert on the subject of love and marriage. His three books on the subject had been translated into seventeen languages and always made the best-seller lists. He was about to undertake a grueling national media tour to promote his latest book, which was dedicated to his wife of ten years and cited their mutual engagement "in the never-ending adventure of marriage."

There was a problem, however. He had been photographed with another woman, a TV personality, an actress known for her seductive roles. The paper in which the photo appeared, a scandal sheet read by millions, implied they'd been having an affair.

I assumed that Paul had come to deal with the issue of the scandal, as he had long since mastered the basic techniques of selling his book on camera. We chatted in my office, and he seemed fairly relaxed. He is a handsome man, charming in the country-squire manner of a young John Huston, and a bit of a flirt. When we had caught up on what he had been doing, I suggested that we go to our studio and conduct an on-camera interview.

I began with the usual questions ("What is your book about?" "What tips do you have for squabbling spouses?") that interviewers ask when they haven't read the book. His easy, bantering mood was replaced at once by agonized uneasiness. His body slumped. He leaned back and twisted in his seat, hanging on to the arm of the chair with one hand until his knuckles went white. I was amazed by the amateurish performance of my former star pupil. Finally, I popped the big one: "You were photographed with a woman, not your wife. An affair was implied. What do you have to say?" He hesitated before he began to stutter. His eyes darted to the side and then avoided contact completely. His breathing sped up, and he took his breath in little gasps. When the denial came out, it was a weak one—full of clichés. "She's an old family friend . . . there was nothing between us."

People say the camera never lies. Actually, what they mean is **the body always tells the truth**. Here was a highly articulate man—a motivational speaker—reduced to a mass of quivering Jell-O by just the mention of a peccadillo, which he fervently denied. It is no wonder videotaped confessions are so condemning. He was wearing a mask of guilt. You could see it in his eyes, his hands, his posture; hear it in his voice; feel it in the air. He simply wasn't telling the truth.

Bear in mind, we were rehearsing for his media tour, which was only a week away. When an author goes out to plug a book, he or she must be prepared like an athlete for a marathon event. It is not unusual for a person to be subjected to as many as seven or eight interviews a day—radio, TV, and print. Then it's on to the next city. Paul's schedule was grueling—three full weeks on the road.

"What is the truth, Paul?" I asked. "Are you having marriage problems?"

He nodded. "Yes."

I felt a sudden surge of sympathy. "How long has this been going on?" I asked.

"Basically, the whole time I was writing the book. God, I feel like such a hypocrite! Here I was espousing fidelity as an absolute necessity when I met this other woman. I was in pain! She was understanding, sympathetic. I didn't think twice."

"Are you still seeing her?"

"No. After the article appeared, we agreed to stop. It caused too much pain. We still talk from time to time. We really *are* friends."

"What about your wife?" I asked.

"We're working on our relationship."

I believed him. More important, I could see he was starting to believe himself. An hour before, he was guilty. Now his true feelings were beginning to emerge. Rather than press on, I gave him some homework: "You need to take a forgiveness walk. Take a walk on the beach and forgive yourself for being human and fallible. You're a good man. You're making a go of it with your wife. As you say in the book, understanding and accepting the way your spouse really is is the key to a marriage's survival. You've come clean with her. As far as the public is concerned, you're the man who wrote the book. They want to hear what you have to say. Reread it, pick out a couple of poignant examples, talk about yourself if you like. It's very moving when you speak from the heart."

The next day he was back. I could tell at once he felt better. "I did what you said. I forgave myself. And if a reporter asks me, I'm not going to lie, but I won't go into the gritty details either."

He was out of the woods.

By forgiving himself, Paul got back to self-acceptance and along the way regained his sense of humor. He pushed through his feelings of guilt and shame and was able once again to feel proud of his achievements. Now that he felt good about himself and knew what he wanted to say, he was ready to face the media.

Forgiveness frees up your feelings. It gives you the room to get in touch with feelings, both good and bad, and gets you out of the trap of always being "good." True feelings are not always sweet or nice. Listen to your body. If you feel a catch in your throat or tightness in your stomach, realize they are valuable signals that something is disturbing you. React, speak up, say your feelings. Become aware when someone is infringing on your boundaries. Be direct. "No" needs to become as comfortable to say as "Yes." Trust your feelings to give you a read on things.

When you are in touch with your feelings, you can decide how to manage them. If someone ignores you, you have a choice whether or not to feel hurt. You can decide if you want to feel angry for three seconds or if you really want to stretch it out. Don't stuff your emotions down, but if you feel pleased, or moved, or sad, or affectionate, let your feelings show. Fear and anger can take up a lot of room inside us. It's important to let these negative emotions out without hurting another person. Then you will create room for good feelings to express themselves.

Knowing that you create your feelings from your thoughts, you always have a choice as to how you react to something. You also have a choice as to how you want to feel. Don't indulge your feelings, but limit and redirect them. Challenge your anger and your fear. First *feel* your feelings, and then *tell* your feelings how to feel.

MOOD CONTAGION

There are all kinds of feelings going around, and moods are contagious. We tend to mimic each other's emotions without even being aware of it. Emotions can be caught by a look, a sigh, or an attitude. Facial expressions, posture, and tone of voice all send signals as to how someone feels. That's why anxiety is a communicable disease. Tension is easily passed from one person to another.

It's easy enough to feel anger on your own. You don't need to pick up another person's anger or pain. Negative feelings are passed just as easily as positive ones. Choose carefully with whom you spend your time. You're looking for the people who are sending "good vibes."

Energy talks in more ways than one. A very sexy young Hollywood actor came to me to get clear about what he wanted to say while on a promotional tour for his soon-to-be-released movie. He sauntered into the studio wearing a light blue workshirt, tight blue jeans, and some old cowboy boots. He moved with a lot of authority right to the talk-show set and sat down. Our cameraman was setting up. I picked up the lavalier microphone. Normally, I would hand the microphone to a client and he would tuck it under his shirt, but this is a very sexy man and I hesitated. I held the mike in my hand and said, "Somebody's got to put this under your shirt." He gave me a smile and said, "Go for it, babe."

I held myself back as something inside my head said, "Get a grip." I felt like Mrs. Robinson in *The Graduate*. He sent out strong signals. Energy talks, literally.

I smiled back and handed him the mike. Just because someone's energy is talking, it doesn't mean you have to respond.

HEART FELT

Abraham Lincoln said, "People are about as happy as they make up their minds to be." For me, it's not so much making up my mind as my heart. My mind can think anything. It has a constant chatter going on inside my head: "I like this. I hate that. You're right. You're wrong." It will judge me in a second on anything I do. And I don't expect this voice to really ever shut up.

My heart is different. That's the place where I am forgiven: where I accept myself as I am and where I have compassion. It's where I see the big picture. Where mistakes are natural.

When my mood is angry or fearful, I feel paralyzed and contracted. Mostly, I feel helpless to change. This is because I have withdrawn my love from myself.

The secret for me is:

I love myself as much as I can from where I am.

Through loving yourself, you create great power because you stop fighting yourself. There is a tremendous healing power in love. Love is energy. When you can open your heart and love yourself just as you are, then you can easily heal the pain and fear inside you. Love is the antidote to all those negative feelings inside you. We can't cut ourselves off completely from our shadow parts. We need them the same way we need physical pain to show us that something is wrong. Any negative feeling we have toward ourselves is showing us a place where we haven't loved ourselves enough.

IMAGINING LOVE EXERCISE

Sit in a comfortable position. Close your eyes and relax yourself. Say this affirmation out loud:

(continued)

I love and accept myself

Imagine that this is totally true. Now get a picture of your chest area right around your heart. Breathe in and out of your heart. Breathe in love, breathe out love. Imagine yourself as totally loved. How do you look when you're loving yourself? How do you act? How do you feel? What do you say to yourself? What do you hear other people saying? Let yourself go. Learn to bask in love.

Nothing outside you can make you whole. If you look to your parents to teach you to love yourself unconditionally, then you may be disappointed. They will inevitably get angry, or be insensitive, or ignore you, and you will not be able to get all the love you need. If you look for love from your peers or spouse, you may also be frustrated and disappointed. That's because ...

Love is an inside job.

You increase your self-love with every choice you make. Ask yourself, "Is this nourishing for me? Will this be a positive experience? Is this a good choice for me?" Feel your worth. Know your value. Honor your feelings, and stand up for yourself. When you do, you find you have a new sense of power.

Love is an active force. It has the power to heal. As you experience more and more love, you will find that you have developed concern and caring not only for yourself but also for others.

Your Star Quality will expand as you learn to trust your feelings and make choices that are good for you. When you no longer live to please others, you let go of all those "I *should* do this" thoughts and you are able to choose what is best for you.

Sometimes it's easier to accept *another's* imperfections than it is to accept our own. I have found by increasing my compassion and love for others that I am able to have more compassion and love for myself. Television and movies are interesting vehicles to use to increase your ability to love. The following exercise shows you how to use these mediums to expand your tolerance.

EXPANDING EMPATHY EXERCISE

Television and movies provide distance for us to see life's drama without being directly involved. It's a lot easier to view objectively a fictional character yelling than it is your own mate. Distance gives us perspective to see another's flaws in a detached way. If you have trouble with pushy, crude people, start watching television and movies filled with these characters. Just watch them. If you see them with detachment, you'll increase your tolerance. Then, when a pushy, crude person steps into your life, you'll be a little more tolerant. You'll find that people who used to anger you may now amuse you.

Watch dramas, or cop shows, or soap operas. When a particular character irritates you, see if you can understand why someone might like this character. You don't have to approve of him or her. Just set aside your snap judgments and expand your point of view.

THOUGHTS AND FEELINGS

The voice inside your head is talking all the time. There's a running commentary going on that tells you how you feel about yourself. Imagine this: What if every thought we had, every word we said to ourselves shaped our attitude—literally told us who we are? Wouldn't you be careful about what you thought and said to yourself?

Good! Because that's exactly what happens. The brain is like a computer; it believes what you say inside your head. It has no way of knowing if the good or bad messages are true. It simply acts on the information that is fed into it. The messages that you put in your head shape your self-concept. Remember: You project what you believe. That's why I can work with one middle-aged, overweight woman who convinces me she is stunning—because she believes it—while another woman of similar physical attributes convinces me she's over the hill because that's what she believes. I have had gorgeous women tell me they think they're unattractive and very average-looking women convince me they were stunning. All projected their beliefs about themselves.

I'll let you in on a secret:

You tell people how they should see you.

This point was illustrated quite clearly when I judged a Miss Hollywood beauty contest. A number of young women—twenty or so—were competing for first prize. The winner would go on to the Miss California pageant.

The three judges were sitting in a large auditorium with about four hundred people; the contestants, all of whom were very attractive, paraded before us on an elevated ramp. When these women started coming down the ramp, I noticed they all were making certain statements about themselves. One woman was walking strangely, and I noticed that her thighs were large. Another woman moved in a way that pointed out how short she was. It was odd. These women were up on a ramp, and it was almost impossible to tell how tall they were—yet, even in high heels, the message from one contestant was "I'm short." Still another woman was smiling awkwardly. There seemed to be something she was trying to hide about her mouth. Without knowing it, each woman was sending a strong message; they were all projecting their beliefs about themselves.

At one point, down the runway came one woman who seemed to feel really comfortable with herself. She moved in a way that said, "I love myself. I have nothing to hide." I didn't pick up on *any* negative thoughts she had about herself. My immediate instinct was "This is Miss Hollywood." I marked her as my first choice on the ballot—and, unbeknownst to me, the other two judges had done exactly the same. When we got into the judges' room to make our decision, we found we had all unanimously chosen the same woman—because she had actually chosen herself.

We all wonder what people think of us, but the truth is, people think about us pretty much what we're thinking about ourselves. You tell people how to feel about you every moment of every day. Once you get comfortable with yourself, you project positive images that other people will pick up from you. Most people have it backward: They think that if others judge them harshly, they will have a negative self-image. That's a lot of baloney. Negative thoughts start from within. Forget about trying to find out who you are from others. *You tell people how to see you.*

The late actress Ruth Gordon explained how this works. As she saw it, "Beauty and courage are the two most admired things in life. Beauty is Vivien Leigh, Garbo; you fall down in front of them. You don't have it? Get courage. It's what we're all in awe of. It's the New York Mets saying, 'We'll make our own luck.' I got courage because I was five-foot-nothing and not showgirl beautiful."

SELF-TALK

If you need to adjust some negative beliefs that you may have, a good place to start is by monitoring your self-talk.

Let me share something with you:

What you say to yourself is more important than what is actually going on in your life.

For example, say you're in a relationship and that person leaves you. You think to yourself, "Oh, my God, he left me. I am so worthless! No one will ever love me again!" Now, what are you doing? What messages are you sending to yourself? Is this what you want to create—a lonely life in which no one ever loves you again? I don't think so. This is where you need to change your negative self-talk. Imagine that your fiancé does leave you. And he leaves you for another woman. Now, what if you say to yourself, "What can I learn from this experience? From this pain? I can change my approach and find someone who appreciates me more." Or say you have a job interview and you think you didn't do very well. You might say to yourself, "If I have a second interview I'll make sure to add the information I left out. If I don't get another shot at this job, at least I've learned from this experience and I'll do better next time."

Now you're talking! You're not blaming yourself; you're not feeding your fears. You're learning from life. And by communicating to yourself this way, you're allowing yourself to grow through your experiences. Top athletes and coaches know the importance of what they say to themselves. They psyche themselves. That's why when Vince Lombardi was asked about his coaching record he said, "I never lost a game. I just ran out of time."

If you've ever exercised and gotten your body in shape, then you know exactly how this works: In order to stay in shape, you need to keep working out. If you stop exercising, your body loses tone. Your mind works *exactly* the same way. Once you *get* your mind in shape, it takes continuous practice to *keep* it in shape.

Self-acceptance comes when you accept *all* of you—the negative and the positive. It's the same with self-talk. We have many voices inside us. Your success in your personal life depends on how well you communicate to yourself and which voices you choose to listen to. As my friend Emily says, "I've got a billion voices . . . they talk to me all the time. Wake up. Do your work. Clean the house. Pay the bills. I envy Joan of Arc. At least she only heard one voice, 'Save France.' "

Self-talk is not just happy talk. Don't make that common mistake. You don't avoid the negative thoughts that pop into your head, you *include* them.

For example, I have a friend who has grown into a powerful public speaker. Yet every time he gets up to make a speech, this little voice inside his head says, "You can't do this. You have no idea what you're going to say. There are hundreds of people in this audience. You're sure to make a fool of yourself. Get out of here now." He recognizes this voice of fear as the scared part of him, the part that does not like to perform in public. So he just says, "Calm down. It's not you who is speaking." And he then allows the powerful public speaker in him to begin talking.

THE CRITIC

One of the noisiest voices we hear is that of the Critic. I have a friend, Patti, who describes her Critic this way: "Every day I get up, put on my cement boots, pummel myself, and proceed to take my Uzi out and eliminate anyone I see. Every day is Jonestown in my life." Years ago, my Critic was not doing much better than hers. Let me just give you some of the powerful messages my Critic used to tell me:

> *Nobody loves you.*
> *You never do anything right.*
> *You're not good enough.*
> *You're stupid.*
> *You don't deserve to be here.*
> *You have nothing to contribute.*
> *You're not attractive enough.*
> *You can't do it.*
> *Don't even try.*
> *You'll never make it.*
> *You don't deserve it.*

I developed this powerful Critic early in my life, as many of us do. We want to please our parents, then our teachers, then our boyfriends or girlfriends, then, once the pattern is set, our husbands, wives, and bosses. If, somehow, we fail to please, then it must be our fault.

The problem for most of us is that our inner Critic plays his part so well. He is designed to focus only on those parts of ourselves that we dislike. The Critic does not spend a lot of time noticing how playful, loving, and compassionate we are. He is trained to see only what is wrong. He has no capacity to be objective or to see the whole picture. Since he won't learn about us—the *real* us—let's learn about him. Let's spend a little time with our Critic.

When you get good at discovering your self-criticizing, you need only notice it and take a breath. It's not that your inner Critic is always wrong. He's not. He's just so seriously judgmental about everything. He needs help so he can lighten up. You start by just "observing" your behavior rather than judging and evaluating everything you do.

LISTENING TO THE CRITIC EXERCISE

Take two hours during the day and notice any time you criticize or judge yourself for anything at all. It could be your appearance, something you said, something you didn't do, being late, how you feel. Anything. Just notice it.

Write it down and say to yourself as you do it, "Criticizing. Criticizing."

Now, notice how these thoughts feel in your body. Do they make you feel looser or tighter? Just watch the process. Notice how you feel. How often do you notice that you criticize yourself? Every few minutes, two or three times an hour? When you don't judge yourself for a while, do you feel differently?

This is an exercise in listening to your mind. Listening to what you say to yourself.

Now, read through your list of judgments. How do they make you feel?

When I first started listening to my Critic, she used to call me names. "Stupid" was a favorite. I learned just to say "Stop." I told myself it was *my* mind and I had every right to think the thoughts I wanted. Eventually, I learned to stop struggling with negative self-judgments. When they cropped up, I countered them with positive thoughts. "You're stupid" became "That's an interesting thought. Let's explore it further and see if it's valid." As a result, my Critic has lightened up quite a lot. She's even gotten much more positive. Now, instead of hearing "I'm a failure," I hear "I'm fine. Another opportunity will come along." Or I hear "I made a mistake. Everyone makes them" instead of "I'm dumb."

Most of us, if we saw a printout of the negative self-talk that goes on in our minds, would be totally shocked. Listening to the voice of the Critic can be a pretty brutal experience. That's why it's important to separate unnecessary negativity from valid self-improvement. The first step is to stop being afraid to fail—at anything. The second step is to understand that a simple mistake does not constitute failure.

MISTAKES

We need to let ourselves make mistakes. This is how life teaches us. No question that you and I are occasionally going to say and sometimes do something stupid. But does that make us stupid? It took me a while to learn that I could do something stupid and all that meant was I had behaved stupidly. My behavior was stupid, but I was not a stupid person. I was a smart person who just happened, in that one moment, to behave stupidly. The key is to avoid repeating the same stupid behavior. As long as I learn from my mistakes, why shouldn't I make them? This sounds simple, but in practice it takes some work to reach that stage. Unfortunately, the Critic is right there ready to make a decision about how bad a mistake it really was.

I keep a stash of cups and plates to help me remind myself that it's okay to make mistakes. If I'm being too hard on myself, I just walk into the kitchen and pick up a plate, drop it, and watch it break. With satisfaction, I say to myself, "I'm allowed to make mistakes." This is usually shocking enough to shut up the Critic and get me back to self-acceptance. I find it's far better to sacrifice a plate or cup than to sacrifice my own peace of mind.

ACCEPTING IMPERFECTION

It always seems easier to accept another's flaws than it is to accept our own. It may be because we have distance from others and we're right on top of ourselves. We go to the mirror looking for the pounds, the wrinkles, the flaws. When we find the imperfection, that's where our attention goes.

For years the way I felt about myself was predicated on my skin condition. If I looked in the mirror and there were no pimples, I had a shot at feeling good that day. Two or more pimples would have me returning to the mirror, makeup in hand, hour after hour. Covering. Covering . . .

I have a friend whose hair is thinning on top. After he styles it, he decides if it is a good hair day or a bad hair day. On bad hair days, he keeps running back to the mirror trying to fold his hair over his bald spot.

It's hard to hide what you see as your inadequacies because if you focus an enormous amount of attention on them, people are often drawn to your area of focus. And all that does is make you even *more* aware of those inadequacies.

You are where your attention takes you.

If you spend your time adjusting, obsessing over, and rearranging your face, hair, or clothes, then that's where your attention gets stuck. Years ago I had to force myself to admit I was constantly fretting about my imperfections. There were so few clear skin days. I was chronically dissatisfied with my appearance. It was time to do something.

THE MIRROR

I needed to heal myself, and I began right where the problem started . . . in the mirror. The mirror was the link between myself and the world. I looked in the mirror, and I saw three cysts. They were big and hard and red. They held my eyes, which moved from one cyst to the other. I felt my self-doubt. The mirror was my enemy. It showed me my ugliness. I was criticizing myself and inviting others to criticize me. I knew I could not see clearly. I left the mirror and started to write, "I, Christen, forgive myself for my cystic acne. I, Christen, forgive myself for my cystic acne." It must have taken thirty or forty times before the tears started to flow. I just kept writing. It was so hard to forgive myself for this embarrassment, for these bumps. I cleared out a lot of pain I was holding and went back to the mirror. My eyes were red and soft. I saw something loving in them. For the first time in I don't know how long, I looked into the mirror and saw my face. My whole face. My pretty face. I saw my whole self, not merely a part of that self. And in that moment, I felt love and compassion for myself. The acne would subsequently clear up one day or it would not, but I would not wait to have clear skin in order to accept myself. From then on, when I looked into the mirror I saw *myself*. I would look into the mirror until I felt in every pore that I was complete and, yes, beautiful. At that point I knew I could look in the mirror and find the reflection of love.

JOLIE-LAIDE

I learned that if your acceptance of yourself stops at your skin, or your hair, or your mouth (or whatever it is that you don't accept), then it will be impossible for you to see yourself, to see the whole you. Imagine being able to see yourself with the eyes of someone who loves you very much. You've heard that beauty is in the eye of the beholder. It's true. If someone loves you, admires you, and praises you, it not only makes you feel good, it can make you feel beautiful. That love you feel doesn't only have to come from a spouse or a parent—it can come *from you*. Go look at yourself in the mirror. Study yourself, see yourself for what you are—and decide right now that this is a very good look for you. Look at yourself and decide you like what you see. The odds are, you're not classically beautiful. Few people are. But once you decide that you love yourself, you will look good—and not *just* to yourself but to the outside world.

Jolie-laide is a French term referring to women who are not beautiful feature by feature. They may even be ugly, but they *present* themselves as beautiful. I know a woman, Barbara, who is over six feet tall, with a large nose, large face, large hands, and large feet. She is not what you would call beautiful or even very attractive, but she is comfortable with herself. She wears her size well. Her hands are always beautifully manicured. Her hair and makeup are always perfect. She presents herself with force. As a result, she is striking. She tells people how to see her. She knows the secret: How we see ourselves determines how others see us.

MODELING SELF-ACCEPTANCE

Some of our outer attributes—age, physical height, hands, among others—are difficult to change. So what's the solution? Simple— they need to be *accepted*.

One of my clients, Brenda, is a large woman, six feet tall, around two hundred pounds. She was never comfortable with her physical size but realized she couldn't shrink herself. So her choice was self-acceptance. I suggested she look around for role models—large women who were comfortable with themselves. This was about the time *Roseanne* hit the airwaves. My client began to watch the show weekly. After about a month, we noticed a definite attitude change. Brenda was delivering one-liners, throwing her weight around, so to speak. She found a role model to help her get comfortable with her size, and she even developed quite a sense of humor in the process.

Age was an issue for another client, Jim, the CEO of a Fortune 1,000 company. We reminded him of the presidential debate in which Walter Mondale hammered Ronald Reagan on his age, trying to make it a liability. Reagan, however, replied that he refused to allow his age to be a matter for debate, commenting that he had no intention of making an issue of his opponent's youth and inexperience. That line certainly helped Reagan, and it helped our CEO. Once Jim thought about the experience he brought to the table, he regained his confidence.

We were having a problem with a client who had a lisp that couldn't be corrected. It had to be accepted. All it took was letting Fred listen to tapes of Winston Churchill—certainly a great orator even though he had a lisp—inspiring the British during World War II. Fred noticed that Churchill even learned to use the lisp to his advantage by intentionally mispronouncing key words. The great Prime Minister was especially fond of making the word "Nazis" sound like "nasties," much to the delight of his countrymen.

When acceptance is your goal, look around. You'll find other people who have already done what you want to do or gone where you want to go. All you need to do is follow them.

BEING COMFORTABLE IN YOUR SKIN

"J'entre bien dans ma peau" is French for being comfortable in your own skin. This comfortableness is one reason why so many "mature" European *femmes* manage to be *fatales* without being physically perfect. They are comfortable with no longer being ingenues and know how to play up their best points. They have no delusions about their lost youth and don't concentrate on their flaws.

Self-acceptance means giving yourself permission to be an original, not a copy of someone else. I never thought you could be too comfortable in your skin until the day we coached a porn star for some promotional radio appearances. One of our trainers said, "Will you please move up to our stage so we can videotape our first interview?" She replied, "You mean clothed? You want me to do it clothed?" He answered, "Yes." She replied, "But I'm much more comfortable nude." After some discussion, he convinced her that the interviewer's comfort was just as important as hers and all interviews would be conducted fully clothed.

A woman with Star Quality shows other people how to see her. Her beauty is not tied to her face or her features. Her beauty is created out of the love she feels for herself. She accepts herself with all her imperfections. She knows it's those very imperfections that make her unique.

My own comfortableness in my skin was tested a few years ago. I flew to New York to train a very successful author for her upcoming publicity tour. I had heard rumors she was a real diva, quite temperamental, so I put together my best "dress-for-success" outfit for our meeting. Unfortunately, I left my overcoat in the taxi on the way to the airport. Realizing I was arriving coatless in New York City on a cold January night, I borrowed a Pan Am blanket from the airline to wrap around my shoulders. The stores were closed, and our coaching session was scheduled for eight o'clock the next morning.

I woke up, dressed, threw the Pan Am blanket shawllike over my suit, and hoped for the best. I tightened the blanket around me as I exited the taxi on this freezing-cold day and rushed for the building. I arrived at the elevator exactly at the same time as the author. We faced each other—she was wearing a huge Blackglama mink coat, I was wearing a blue polyester Pan Am blanket. Rather incredulously, she asked, "Are you Christen Brown?" She clearly was hoping that she was addressing someone else who just happened to look like my picture. I smiled and introduced myself. She said, "It's a pleasure to meet you," and looked me over. I could read her thoughts. She seemed to be thinking, "Is this ya-hoo going to tell me something I don't already know?" I said, "You wrote a fascinating book." But what I *didn't* say was "Soon you'll realize my work has nothing to do with how I look." We arrived at her publisher's corporate offices and got to work positioning her book for major best-sellerdom.

I never mentioned leaving my coat in Los Angeles. I never apologized for the blanket because the covering outside had nothing to do with the power I had inside. I may have been in a blanket, but I was also in my element, coaching, empowering, teaching. The postscript is that the book was a megahit. It sold close to one million copies.

INNER ACCEPTANCE

Your beliefs are what create your life. Beliefs are powerful because they make things happen. That's why it's crucial that you change any **destructive** or **disempowering** beliefs into new **self-supporting** ones that will empower you.

I had a client who was working way too hard, putting himself under so much pressure that when I scratched the surface of his beliefs, he eagerly volunteered: "Life's a struggle." I could see he was spending *his* life just proving his point. What if he changed this belief to "Life gives me many interesting challenges." With this new belief, he could let go of his struggle.

Another executive was referred to me by his boss because he couldn't get along with his coworkers. He was very combative. After we had worked together a short time, he mentioned his belief that "it's a dog-eat-dog world." With this in mind, naturally he went for the throat. His belief kept him in an attack-ready mode. What if he changed his belief to "You get out of life what you put into it." He'd have a completely different take on things, wouldn't he?

You must let go of old beliefs if they result in a self-destructive attitude. Beliefs create attitudes, and attitudes shape our behavior. Look at it this way: Who would you like to spend time with—a woman who believes "Life is a bowl of cherries" or one who thinks "Life is the pits"?

Beliefs

Letting go of distorted, limited beliefs is very freeing. And it's not as hard as you might think. Often, people hold on to them merely out of habit. Motivational coach Tony Robbins had a dramatic way of changing limiting beliefs. He taught people to fire-walk across hot coals. He figured if you do one thing you think is impossible, it will cause you to rethink all your limiting beliefs.

The first limiting belief I discovered I had was that whenever someone raised his or her voice to object to or disagree with something I had said, I believed he or she was going to try to convince me I was a bad person. *"If you yell at me, I must be bad." That was my belief.* But when I realized my error, I was able to change. Now, whenever someone gets upset and raises his or her voice, I no longer assume I've done something wrong.

We have beliefs about career, family, money, love, and a myriad of other things that may not be working for us. One of my friends was having lots of trouble going back to work after she started her family. She wanted to continue her career, but something always got in her way. After a short conversation, we uncovered her belief that "a woman can't be successful at both family and career." Since she already had a family, her belief made it impossible for her to have a successful career. If she wanted to change her belief, she herself would have to change and accept that a woman *could* have both a successful family life and an equally successful career.

We get emotionally hooked into our beliefs. Look at religion. People hold such strong religious beliefs that they kill each other in the name of those beliefs. So if you have created a belief that you find doesn't work for you, use your emotion-backed energy to break through the old belief system. My friend did just that with her belief that she couldn't have both a family and career. She got mad. She called me one day and said, "I'm sick of being trapped at home. I'm a smart woman with a college degree; I'm going to prove to myself that I can balance a family and a career." She faced her limiting belief head-on and made a strong decision to change her life. Now she works as a successful freelance writer and can't believe how simple it is to have both a family *and* a career.

If you're feeling doubts or fear about doing something, you may be stuck with a limiting belief—though you may be unaware of it. Another friend and I were discussing beliefs one day. She pointed out that I seemed to be suffering from a belief that says, "I don't get what I want." We went over all the areas of my life in which I had *close* to what I wanted but not *exactly* what I wanted. And I realized I *did* believe that I didn't get what I wanted. An even more startling realization was that if I didn't ever get what I wanted, I would have *justification* for keeping myself permanently bent out of shape. My belief—as subconscious as it was—justified a myriad of upsets in almost every area of my life. Right then and there I decided to dis-create this belief.

Here is what I did:

Since I'd created this belief, I figured I could dis-create it just as easily. So every time I observed myself getting upset about not getting what I wanted, I created enough detachment and distance so I could watch myself reacting. I didn't judge my upset. After all, I was only acting out old programming, following an old belief from the past. I watched this belief upset me for several days until I was sufficiently disgusted to make a change. I decided that I wanted to make a different choice. My new belief would be **"I always get just what I need to learn and grow."** This was a big change for me. It required a lot of trust—self-trust—to imagine that I was, in fact, getting what I needed. What would happen to those upsets, to the rush of anger, to the hissy fits I was so good at throwing? It was daunting work to make such a change, and not a job for the fainthearted. What saved me was another equally strong belief: **"The purpose of life is to grow."** This new belief echoed my already-in-place philosophy. So now, each time I saw myself trying to return to the old belief that "I don't get what I want," I was able to gently remind myself: **"I always get what I need."** And thus I could keep growing.

It's a process. You change beliefs day to day, situation to situation, problem to problem. I know now that you always have a choice. Letting go of limiting beliefs is tremendously empowering work. When we take responsibility for our lives and for what happens to us, then, if we don't like something, we can change it.

"I'm a failure" and "I'm unworthy" are global judgments that can usually be reduced to something simple like "I didn't handle that situation well." Letting go of limiting beliefs and replacing them with empowering beliefs is essential to developing Star Quality.

Answer the following question with "yes," "sometimes," or "no":

"Are you enjoying your life?"

"Yes" indicates a good attitude. "Sometimes" means you live in a so-so world—sometimes good, sometimes bad. "No" indicates you are, by your attitude, attracting a lot of negative situations to yourself. The world is a looking glass; it looks back at us exactly as we look at it. How you want the world to look is entirely up to you.

AUTOSUGGESTIONS AND AFFIRMATIONS

When I realized that we all project how we feel about ourselves, I felt a real responsibility to deal with my issues of self-worth. I kept thinking, "Who wants to be around someone who doesn't believe in herself? Someone who thinks she's stupid or unimportant?" Not me. I want to be with people who love themselves and think they're great—because I want to love myself and think *I'm* great.

I started by taking responsibility for what was going on in my head. I read a lot and discovered that the subconscious mind is where beliefs are stored. That was great news because *the subconscious mind*, I found, *will believe anything you tell it if you tell it long enough and strongly enough.*

Jim Carrey is a good example of what can happen when visualization and autosuggestion are combined with talent and hard work. About seven years ago, when Carrey was an out-of-work actor, he used to drive up Mulholland Drive, park his car, and look out at the lights of Los Angeles. He would say, "I am a popular actor, and every director wants to work with me." Carrey would stay up there until he actually *believed* this was true. Then he would drive down the mountain feeling like he was the biggest star in Hollywood. About this time, Carrey wrote himself a check for $10,000,000 due and payable by Thanksgiving 1995 for "acting services rendered." It was in early 1995 that he made a deal for $10,000,000 to star in the sequel to *Ace Ventura, Pet Detective.* Carrey had talent, and when he added visualization and autosuggestion he turned himself into a powerful comedy star.

The subconscious mind believes what the conscious mind tells it, which is both good and bad news. The bad news is that it's easy for negative, destructive thoughts to root and take hold. The good news is that it's possible to dig those roots up, throw them away, and replace them with positive, life-enhancing thoughts. Obviously, all I had to do was take a look at my life to know I had been putting some pretty negative messages into my subconscious mind. I realized that if I could give my subconscious mind a new idea, one that was clearly stronger, with more emotion and more emphasis, then I could change any of my negative beliefs about myself. This was an exciting discovery, not only for me but for many of my clients who came to us with the opening comment "I hate speaking in public." We immediately changed that comment to "Up until now, I didn't like speaking in public, but now I am learning to enjoy public speaking."

I started reading everything I could on autosuggestion—the best way to reach into your subconscious and inject positive thoughts.

I soon found that when I used autosuggestion and worked with affirmations, I could help myself create a new point of view.

AUTOSUGGESTION RULES

1. *Choose only one specific area* for self-improvement, and work on that until you feel some change.

2. *Keep your suggestions close to reality.* When you are dealing with a physical condition, you can't say, "My ankle is strong and healthy" if it's broken. Say instead "Each day my leg grows stronger and healthier."

3. *Use the present tense.* Always put the idea together as if it were already an accomplished fact: "I am calm and poised." The key phrases are I AM . . . IT IS . . . I FEEL . . .

4. *Move toward something.* Say "I am calm and relaxed." Not "I am nervous." Always create a picture of yourself feeling and acting the way you want to.

5. *Use simple words* that are exciting and emotional such as "I feel vibrant and filled with energy." *Powerful, abundant,*

(continued)

exciting, joyous, and *loving* are all words that touch your sub-conscious or feeling mind.

6. *Take it easy.* Let the suggestion take hold rather than try to make it or force it to happen. Autosuggestion needs to be done from a place of positive expectancy and trust. Use rep-etition, but it's your conviction and the emotion you feel that creates the change in belief for you.

7. *Say it with feeling.* It's emotion-backed energy that makes your words come alive.

The first affirmation I chose to work with was *"I can do any-thing I make up my mind to do."* I figured this would set the tone for lots of positive change.

First, I looked for places where I could legitimately and realis-tically have this feeling. I knew that affirmations have to be emotion-powered, so one of the best places for me to say this af-firmation was in exercise class. I said it silently to myself during leg lifts, and I said it with feeling. During the aerobic dance por-tion of the class, I said to myself, "I CAN DO ANYTHING." I soon found myself getting higher and higher and actually experi-encing the feeling of power that you have when you *know* you can do anything. I repeated this new affirmation before I went to bed at night and again when I woke up in the morning—always saying it with feeling and believing what I was saying.

It takes twenty-one days to change a habit. That's not a scien-tific measurement, of course, and clearly it's open to change de-pending on the individual and the habit, but it's a realistic approximation. It took me about three weeks before I had the feel-ing inside me that I *could* do anything, before it was an ingrained part of my subconscious. And once it was there, I knew I could keep it there forever. It's energy that drives affirmations. It works like this: *Hope* you get something. Now *anticipate* that you'll get it. Then *expect* you'll get it. Feel the difference? Affirmations work when you *expect* they will work.

For my next affirmation, I decided to go for the feeling "*I am enough.*" Feeling incomplete had always been a problem for me. I always needed to be more—brighter, prettier, cleverer—you name it. I had a core belief that I was just not good enough to succeed. I knew I would have to replace it with an even stronger belief that I AM ENOUGH, but I didn't know what "enough" felt like. So I affirmed I AM ENOUGH and added I FEEL GOOD.

It wasn't easy. When I began this process, there were many moments when I felt like I *wasn't* enough and I *didn't* feel good. It definitely started out as a lie. So I realized I had to move myself to a place where I *could* feel good, where I could *experience* being enough and thus allow the belief of I AM ENOUGH to take hold energetically.

Walking had always been something I liked to do. So I tried walking out in nature. I would hike into the mountains and say, "I FEEL GOOD. I AM ENOUGH." The fresh air and nature gave me the good feelings I was looking for. I had no trouble believing myself now because I was telling the truth. I did feel good. My emotion matched my affirmation. I even designed a video exercise to help me. Here's how it works.

This is a video you can play back whenever you want to reinforce this belief. When I played it back, I felt good. I felt like I was enough.

AFFIRMATION VIDEO EXERCISE

You will need: A video camera

(continued)

Instructions: Set up your video camera on a tripod or table. Focus it so you can stand and see yourself from the waist up. Now start taping yourself saying your affirmation. Start with the emotional tone that you feel right now. For example, if you choose to say, "I AM ENOUGH AND I FEEL GOOD," say it with feeling. Move your hands for emphasis. Add energy by moving your body around. I recommend putting on the James Brown recording of "I Feel Good" and moving to it. Throw yourself into the affirmation of "I FEEL GOOD . . . I AM ENOUGH." Be enthusiastic, and say it with feeling.

For the affirmation "I have plenty of time for everything," I recommend you put on a tape of rhythmic, slow music—like Enya's *Watermark* album. Move slowly as you affirm, "I have plenty of time for everything." Stop and enjoy a painting or a picture. Sit down. Have a cup of coffee or tea. *Feel* that you have plenty of time for everything.

A good time to work on the affirmation "I have radiant health and vitality" is when you're doing your exercise program. Say this affirmation while on the treadmill, when you're walking, or as you do your yoga exercises. As you stretch, move, and sweat, get the feeling of radiant health. Experience your vitality. Say it: "I have radiant health and vitality."

A list of self-support affirmations appears at the end of this chapter. Here are some of my favorites. Make up your own list of top ten affirmations.

You need to use words and expressions that are meaningful to you. Change the words to suit yourself, but keep them simple and work with only one affirmation at a time. You must use your emotions to get you to a place where you're not just saying the words but believing them. Say them out loud, write them, videotape and audiotape yourself saying them with feeling. A good way to say an affirmation is in front of a mirror while looking right into your own eyes.

Let all your negative thoughts or feelings come up. When you hear yourself saying something like "I know it won't work," cancel that thought and instead try saying, "Let me see, this could work." Move through your limiting thoughts. Use your affirmations until your affirmations become you. What we affirm today we create tomorrow.

MY TOP TEN AFFIRMATIONS

1. I'm having a great day.
2. I feel good.
3. Life is good.
4. I am easygoing.
5. It's okay to have what I want.
6. I have plenty of time for everything.
7. Challenges help me grow.
8. Life is so interesting.
9. I am strong and well.
10. I am filled with energy.

THE SELF

After several months of using autosuggestion and doing inspired affirmations, I realized there was another voice inside me. This voice was very different from my Critic. It gave me helpful messages and a whole other perspective on life. Affirmations, I realized, were key to opening up this voice I call the Self. The Self is objective and nourishing, rather like a good mother. The Self tells me life-affirming, funny, and empowering things. She coaches me to lighten up, to get distance from a situation and not take things so seriously. She makes up rhymes and sees humor all over the place. Yesterday I was walking to lunch singing "I can do anything" to the tune of Smokey Robinson's "I Would Do Anything." That's the Self talking. Here are some of the things she regularly says to me:

> *I am powerful.*
> *I am loving.*
> *I am perfect.*
> *I am smart.*
> *Life is good.*
> *I am healthy.*
> *I am contributing greatly to life.*
> *I have lots of time to do everything.*
> *I always have whatever I need.*

Now this is a voice I love to hear from. She is the one who helps me keep things in perspective. If I start to get upset, I usually hear the voice saying, "So what? It's not important. Let it go."

The Self is very affirming and life-giving. But I've only been hearing from her in the last few years. She appeared only after I was able to clear out much of my self-doubt and self-criticism; she came only after I learned to forgive myself and accept myself as I am. I view the true Self-talk that I hear now as a kind of gift, one that came after all the work I did on myself.

Here's an exercise I designed for someone who kept saying, "I don't like myself when I lose my temper and attack someone, and I don't like myself when I don't speak up, and I don't like myself when I talk fast." Those negatives just went on and on. Realizing her Critic was out of control, I explained to her that she really didn't dislike herself. What she disliked was her *behavior*. That's very different. You *can* change your behavior. And it's important to understand that *you are not your behavior*.

STOPPING BEHAVIOR EXERCISE

When you find an area of your behavior that is irritating to you, just say:

I don't like that behavior.
That's not me.

For instance, if you don't like yourself when you lose your temper and attack someone, then say:

I don't like that behavior.
That's not me.
I am in control of my temper.
I'm not a person who attacks other people. If I lose my temper, I take a walk. I get control of myself. I don't communicate until I can speak calmly and clearly.

Okay, now you've got your affirmations and you're using auto-suggestion, but negative thoughts keep creeping in, thoughts like "I'll never get a better job" or "I can't lose weight." It's natural to have those thoughts, but you certainly don't want to program that amazing computer, your brain, with them. So I use this simple technique:

Don't fight the negative thoughts, *just replace them with ones that work better for you.* Say "I am confident of my abilities" instead of "I'll never get a better job." Or instead of "I can't lose weight," say "My body is becoming slender and strong" or even "I like the weight I am now."

I've got one more powerful point to share with you:

You can act yourself into a new way of thinking.

Or in the Hollywood vernacular, "Fake it until you make it."

ACT AS IF

It is just as easy to "act" yourself into a new way of thinking as it is to "think" yourself into action. In experiments, even people who *fake* high self-esteem begin feeling better about themselves. By merely going through the motions and acting "as if," you can trigger the emotions so you can act yourself into a new way of thinking. For example, recent research has shown us that you don't just smile when you feel good. The reverse is also true. When you smile you actually feel better. This is an ACT AS IF in action. And what's interesting is that an ACT AS IF works whether you believe it or not.

Here's how I've used it for clients who want to make a change. Let's say you're afraid of new situations. You don't like entering a room filled with people you've never met and making small talk. There's a cocktail party coming up and you won't know anyone there. You have to attend. It's business, and your boss expects you to represent your company.

You're very nervous. Then, you remember you have seen people walk into a room at a cocktail party and introduce themselves to strangers. It's even happened to you—a stranger has come over and started up a conversation. You start to think how you would do this.

ACT AS IF EXERCISE

What if I ACT AS IF I am a person who is comfortable introducing herself at parties and making small talk? First, I will enter the room and look for a place where people are congregating, either at the food table or the bar. Then I will order something to drink and look for a person at the bar to talk to. If there is no one there, I'll move on to the food. First, I'll make a comment about the room or the decorations, just to break the ice. Then I'll talk about something related to this group.

It's very easy. Once you see yourself as someone who can introduce herself to strangers at parties, you'll find you can become a person who is comfortable in new situations. It was Plato who said, "Act an attribute and it will be yours." People have been using this concept for thousands of years. It has a very good chance of working for you. It must be obvious by now that . . .

Confidence is an inside job.

When you understand this, you should be willing to do the work to master power and presence. It all starts with you. This chapter is filled with tools to help you make important attitude adjustments, but *you* are the only one who can make these exercises come alive. What you tell yourself becomes a belief. That's why daily self-coaching works. You need to become your own life coach.

SELF-COACHING

Like every smart coach, you need a game plan. Pep talks and affirmations are key. Your inner voice sets the tone for handling difficult situations. Positive Self-talk gives you the support you need to handle intense situations.

Take control of your thoughts and focus on your inner dialogue. For instance, if you need to handle an aggressive person, calm yourself by saying, "He's angry. This could upset me. I'll calm myself by doing my rhythmic breathing. Then I can find out what's upsetting him and solve the problem."

Pep Talks

Pep talks are a function of self-coaching. They help you get yourself in the right frame of mind. When I wake up in the morning, I go to the mirror and give myself a pep talk. It sounds like this:

PEP TALK EXERCISE

"I'm alive. Look at me [big smile]. I'm going to have a great time today. I'm going to . . .": (choose one or all)

Enjoy myself
Do good work
Eat healthy
Own this day
Make lots of money

Get specific about what you want to accomplish.

I like pep talks so much I've included some for different situations.

Pep-Talk Examples

You've been invited to a surprise party at a friend's home. Many people you've never met will be attending. As you approach the door, you are overwhelmed by nerves and anxiety. Rather than panic and run away, take a few long, deep breaths and give yourself a pep talk:

"I'm an interesting person. People at this party will want to meet me. I like meeting people as much as they like meeting me. This is going to be fun!"

A friend has set you up on a blind date. Since you have not dated for a while, you are understandably nervous. You've heard many wonderful things about the man you'll be meeting. How will you possibly measure up? Give yourself a pep talk to lift your spirits to the level they belong:

"This is very exciting. I'm looking forward to meeting this new person, and I'm a worthwhile person to meet as well. I want to find out all about (The person's name) **. I'm going to enjoy this experience to the fullest."**

You've just started a new business and have met someone who wishes to contract for your services. You discuss the woman's needs and finally discuss pricing. When you tell her your price, she flinches. "That's quite a lot, don't you think?" she asks. You answer "No," but internally you begin to question your policies and your price. You check your competition and find that your prices are competitive. You need to get back to her with a quote. A pep talk right now is just what you need:

"My work is important, and my service is valuable to lots of

people. I am charging a fair price, and it is well worth the money. I value myself and my talents and feel good about my work. I'm going to be very successful, and I feel great knowing that."

Here's a pep talk you may want to use to cheer yourself on:

"___(Your name)___, you know how to be successful. You have talent. You are just naturally good with people. You deserve to have everything you want. I love you. I believe in you. You shine just like a star."

Use the pep talks that meet your needs. If none of these are exactly right, be creative and design a pep talk that works for you.

AFFIRMATIONS

Along with pep talks, affirmations are an effective way to self-coach. If you're going to talk to yourself, here are some things you may want to say and an exercise that helps you say them. The ones that give you the most trouble, the ones you really dislike, are probably the ones you need to be working with the most. You can say them with your inner voice, but it's much stronger to say them out loud with authority and enthusiasm.

AFFIRMATIONS EXERCISE

You will need: An audio tape recorder.

Instructions: Of all the voices you listen to daily, the most influential is your own. Your inner voice defines how you respond to situations. Let's add some powerful options by choosing self-supportive affirmations from the following list.

Choose the affirmation(s) you want to concentrate on first, and then get to work. Make a tape recording of your voice saying your affirmation(s) with enthusiasm. Use your own words. Give yourself these new messages loud and clear.

Put this tape in the tape deck in your car or listen to it at home, and feel the truth of these words.

Self-Supportive Affirmations

I love and accept myself.
I am worthy.
I am a lot of fun to be with.
I express myself freely.
I love to share myself with others.
It is safe to let my beauty show.
I am participating 100 percent in my life.
I am taking risks.
My life is a fulfilling and joyful experience.
I am unique.

I am confident.

I am competent.

I can do anything I want to do.

The more I give, the more I receive.

I am the creator of my life.

I am accepting my creativity and letting it flow.

I am content.

I feel warm and loving toward myself and others.

I am confident in my abilities.

I welcome every challenge that life brings me.

Life is meant to be exciting and joyful.

I am good.

Life is to be enjoyed.

Success is being happy with myself.

I am intelligent.

I have good ideas.

I learn from my mistakes.

I love and accept my body.

I desire to eat food that is good for me.

I am eating less and enjoying it more.

I have radiant health and vitality.

I take care of my body, and it takes care of me.

I am attractive.

I own this day.

I am grateful for my life.

I have been blessed with many gifts.

I use problems as an opportunity to grow.

I would rather be me than anyone else in the world.

Life is a gift.

Pep talks and affirmations are helpful—but keep in mind that they are only words unless you move yourself into a place of emotionally charged belief. Your attitude is what determines who you are, how you relate to others, and how others relate to you. It all starts with *you.* If your attitude isn't in the right place and you start to walk into a room, turn around and walk out. Do not even bother to enter the room because *if you are not getting what you need from yourself, you won't get what you need from someone else.*

To change your attitude, practice the following:

Self-Forgiveness
Autosuggestions/Affirmations
ACT AS IFS
Pep Talks

And walk back through the door with your Star Quality showing.

CHAPTER FOUR

You're Only as Big as You Think You Are

What you see is what you get.
—FLIP WILSON

This entire chapter is devoted to the outside, to your outer show. Clients have said to me rather self-righteously, "I am as God made me," implying that no improvements were necessary. Or as one woman put it, "Isn't it best to be myself, warts and all?" I answered, "Probably not. Given the choice, it's better to be yourself minus the warts." We are all given a certain amount of raw material. What we end up with is up to us.

Thanks to video technology and instant playback, it is possible to watch yourself being you. And thanks to video feedback, it is equally possible to make changes in the way you come across, to strengthen the way you present yourself, to become a more confident you.

You are going to learn techniques—many of which are already practiced by successful people very much in the public eye—that will dramatically improve the impression you make on people in your own world. This chapter is designed to bring your carriage, body language, facial expressions, and voice to Star Quality level. Much of what we will be doing will be making purely mechanical changes in your outer presentation. The video exercises will guide you along the way.

OUTER SELF-ACCEPTANCE

We are visual creatures and, like it or not, we judge things by their visual impact. The hair, cosmetics, and fashion industries are built on our obsession with our looks. That's why people make their first impression in only seven seconds. It takes only that long to get a visual impression, good or bad. So let's deal with this outer self and create an appearance that you like and can accept. You don't have to look like a hunk or a model. You simply have to be comfortable with the way *you* look.

Beauty for me has always been something of a self-creation. We are all born with a certain natural beauty. You have limitations, I have limitations. We all do. Coco Chanel put it bluntly: "Anyone past the age of twenty who looks in the mirror to be pleased is a fool. You see the flaws, not the beauty. Beauty is charm."

True stars are aware of their individual appeal. Many stars are comfortable with their imperfections and appreciate themselves as they are. Barbra Streisand could have had her nose bobbed, but wasn't interested. When Clark Gable was told he could never be a star with his ears sticking out, he declined to have them pinned back.

Other celebrities enjoy changing and improving their looks. Dolly Parton is refreshingly open about self-improvement through plastic surgery. She writes, "I've had nips and tucks and trims and sucks, boobs and waist and butt and such, eyes and chin and back again, pills and peels and other frills and I'll never graduate from collagen."

Beauty is not created part by part. It is all of your parts working together that creates your beauty. It makes no difference if your feet are too large or your neck is too short. When you accept *all* of you, you appreciate your own unique, unduplicable self. It is then that you realize beauty is created out of self-appreciation and self-love.

If you realize this and are still not comfortable with something that can be corrected or improved, you have two choices: Change it or accept it. One woman I know has a mole on her face, very near her mouth. It is large and noticeable. When I asked her if it bothered her, she replied, "Certainly not. This is a family mole. My mother has this exact mole and my grandmother before her. Why would I remove a part of who I am?" This made perfect sense to me. She wasn't trying to hide her mole. In fact, she saw it as giving her character.

A family nose. A family mole. If it has significance for you, if you honor a physical attribute as part of who you are, then you accept it and it doesn't detract from how you feel about yourself. If, however, you have a large bump on your nose that has no significance for you and even bothers you when you look at it, then you may want to consider a change.

Here's how this worked for me. I enjoy change and have no reservations about making changes in my outer appearance. In fact, I love improving my appearance. It all started with the crossed eyes I had as a child. After two years of going to a vision therapist twice a week, my eyes straightened out. And I got it: You *can* change how you look. Crossed eyes can be straightened; pimples can be cleared up; crooked teeth can be fixed. The possibilities are endless. From the age of thirteen on, I have improved my appearance.

From braces to a chemical peel to remove acne scars to plastic surgery to remove a bump on my nose, I improved my looks. I practiced yoga to firm my muscles and began to like the way I looked. I realized something important:

It's difficult to dislike your face or body and still like yourself.

My body and my face are not perfect, and neither are yours. But we are all unique. There are no other faces or bodies in the world exactly like yours. They belong only to you. And if you want to be confident from the inside out, then you need to take a look at yourself and decide what needs to be changed and what needs to be accepted.

Let's take a look in the camera, first alone and then with a friend. Take a look at yourself and make some decisions. Any outer changes you want to make should be acknowledged now. I must warn you, it can be shocking when you first start seeing yourself on camera. As one of my clients asked, "I know this sounds crazy, but am I the person I see on the TV screen or the person I think I am?" I explained that he had discovered the power of the video camera. It shows us ourselves as we are *and* as others see us.

Keep in mind that what is important to one person may mean nothing to another. I have had clients with huge bags under their eyes insist that those bags gave them character, while others with a slight puffiness have charged to the plastic surgeon.

Do this next exercise. Review the tape. If your decision is to change something, then get advice from at least three competent professionals—for example, a trainer, a hairstylist, or a plastic surgeon—before you make any changes. Any change you make, small or large, from hairstyle to cosmetic surgery to weight reduction, must be done responsibly.

CAMERA EYE VIDEO EXERCISE

You will need: A video camera
A chair
A quiet room

Instructions: Set the camera on a tripod or on a table facing you. Frame the shot from your chest up. Turn on the camera. Take a seat. Sit and look into the camera. Just look into the camera eye. Don't say anything. When you feel comfortable, slowly turn your head to one side and then the other. Let the camera "see you." Smile. Stop the tape. Rewind the tape and sit and watch the playback. You can put the tape on Pause and watch it over again.

Stand up and move the camera far enough back so it can see your whole body. Tape yourself front, side, and back. Play back the tape and evaluate your general appearance. Assess your face, hair, and body. If you decide you want to make a change, ask a friend you respect and trust to watch the tape with you. See if he or she agrees with your changes. Remember that anything you aren't going to change or improve needs to be accepted.

THE SEVEN KEYS

The following areas are what I call the Seven Keys. Working with them will unlock any blocks you may have to a strong outer presentation.

1. Physical presence
2. Gestures
3. Facial expressions
4. Eye contact
5. Touch
6. Voice
7. Rapport

As you strengthen and improve each area of expression, you will find it much easier to radiate Star Quality presence.

PHYSICAL PRESENCE

The way you walk into a room makes a strong statement about you. If your posture or walk needs correcting, take the time to empower your physical presence.

I remember the first day I met Mary. She walked with her head slightly bowed, her shoulders rounded. When she stood to meet me, she slumped down into herself. Because she came to me for presence work, she was highly motivated to learn our body alignment and presence and power walk techniques. Mary wanted to walk into a room and be noticed. But before we could work on her walk, we explained that she needed to learn body alignment. You need a posture that lets you feel "up on things," like you're being pulled up—exactly the opposite of what was happening to Mary.

We showed Mary how to distribute her weight evenly on the balls of her feet, hold her rib cage high, and tuck her pelvis under it. Once she had a balanced stance, we showed her how to straighten her head.

Mary now has physical presence. When I look at her, I get the feeling she is in touch with every little vertebrae. She walks with purpose and conveys an inner assurance. What a remarkable change she made in her physical presence—and it all started with posture.

Here's what we told her:

If your chin is cocked upward (think of William Buckley), you are conveying a superior, and possibly arrogant, tone. If your head is bowed or cocked downward, however, you are projecting an inferior tone. What you want to establish is a neutral position, with your chin cocked neither up nor down, but kept level. Start with our body alignment exercise.

BODY ALIGNMENT EXERCISE

You will need: A full-length mirror

Instructions: Stand approximately three feet back from the mirror. Plant your feet to give you a firm base. Space them so they are comfortably placed beneath your shoulders.

Now stand sideways in front of the mirror. Bend your knees slightly. Notice if your pelvis and buttocks are out of alignment with your back. Notice if your head juts forward.

Put your hands on your hips and gently roll your pelvis forward, which allows your stomach to move in more. Stand up. Your buttocks should be tucked in slightly. To align your head, pull your chin in slightly. (Your chin is cocked neither up nor down; it is level.) Your chest should be high and your shoulders settled comfortably on your frame. Imagine a string running up your spine, through your trunk, and out through the center of your head. This is your invisible balance point.

Now that Mary knew how to stand tall, she commented that she felt more confident. This is natural because if you stand with your buttocks tucked in and your chest high, head erect, you feel far more energized. You transmit a bearing of confidence.

The point here is:

Change your physiology and you change your state of mind.

Just by doing something as simple as straightening your back, or your walk, or even changing the way you cock your head, you add power to your physical presence.

Body Energizer

I like to do this body energizer technique in our workshops. I have participants sit down, slump over, and act tired. They sit and breathe that way for a minute, long enough to get the feeling of being bored.

Then I say, "Now sit up with your rib cage high and your head erect. Act energized." Notice the difference. Just by changing your physiology, you change your point of view. Research has shown us that when you mimic the outward signs of a mood, you can induce that mood. If you want to feel depressed, slump over, let your head hang down, and start yawning. Now just wait. Sitting up with a bright look on your face will definitely add power to your physical presentation.

Also, you have up to 30 percent more energy standing as opposed to sitting. So stand up and get ready to take a walk.

Walks

Let's start by taking a look at your walk and seeing what it says about you.

WALKING VIDEO EXERCISE

You will need: A video camera

Instructions: Set your video camera far enough back so that it can pick up your walk—about twelve feet from you. Either ask a friend to shoot it, or put the camera on a tripod and videotape yourself walking. Pick up your stride, your arm movement, and the quickness of your walk.

Now rewind the tape and watch it with a friend. Answer these questions: Is your walk slow or quick? Is your head level or facing down? Do you pick your feet up, or do they shuffle along? Do your arms swing, or do they stay at your side?

Your walk says a great deal about you. Look at the way actors adopt poor posture and awkward moves to portray characters. The hangdog way Dustin Hoffman moved as Ratso Rizzo in *Midnight Cowboy* was dramatically different from the way he moved as a young student just out of college in *The Graduate*. What happened to his walk when he changed genders in *Tootsie*? Or when he played an autistic man in *Rain Man*? Your stance and walk are the first places you communicate how you feel about yourself. The way you move gives people a good idea of how to see you. Susan Strasberg, daughter of legendary acting coach Lee Strasberg, was walking unnoticed through New York City with Marilyn Monroe. Suddenly, Monroe stopped and asked, "Would you like to see Marilyn Monroe?" Susan answered a surprised "Yes." Marilyn then proceeded to take off her scarf and put on her

Marilyn Monroe walk. Within minutes, fans were swarming around her. She knew exactly how to project Marilyn Monroe . . . she told people how to see her.

I have screened tapes of hundreds of people walking: in a shopping mall, at the airport, in a factory. You would be amazed how much a person's walk can tell you about how he feels about himself. A rigid, controlled military stance, a sexy hip-swaying walk, an overconfident swagger, a hunched-over shuffle all make dramatically different comments about a person.

There are lots of walks to choose from. I'd like you first to try this one:

The Old Walk

To see how a walk can actually affect your state of mind, try this one—you'll immediately know how it feels to appear old, tired, or depressed. Start by shuffling your feet. Just sort of drag them across the floor. Bend your body over slightly. Now keep your head down, and look at your shoes. Take short strides. Pin your arms to your sides. Don't forget to move slowly. Feel tired yet? Keep going. You will.

Now let's try two walks that will *help* you.

The Presence Walk

You want a loose, relaxed, open feeling to your movement. An uptight military walk can be stiff and stressful. Rhythm and movement are essential to a strong walk. Feel the vitality that comes from using the presence walk.

After you have a good experience of the presence walk, you're ready to put some force behind it.

PRESENCE WALK EXERCISE

Use your body alignment technique. Pull up your chest and let your shoulders settle on your frame. Look straight ahead. Take comfortable strides. Let your arms swing naturally. This walk flows in a relaxed rhythm.

The Power Walk

I first used the power walk to help one of our clients who was having difficulty learning to move with power and presence. Beth was the sweetest woman. She loved to please. Her walk, her smile, her head nods all showed her soft, gentle nature. The problem was she was having a difficult time commanding respect in the world. Because she was so acquiescent, people just pushed her around. Her walk seemed a good place to start. She was used to sneaking into a room, head down, feet shuffling along. We showed her our body alignment exercise and coached her on the presence walk. She practiced it diligently, and, after several weeks, it was time to test her walk for results. I designed this exercise to test her walk's power.

Beth reported back to me that the first time she did the power walk exercise, she took herself from our On Camera studio in West Los Angeles right over to Rodeo Drive in Beverly Hills. She had practiced her walk for weeks and was comfortable with the affirmations "I HAVE POWER. I HAVE PRESENCE." She told me, "When I first started my walk, I saw some pretty intense people coming at me, and my instincts told me to move aside. But that was not what I was working on. I had been moving aside my whole life, making room for everyone else. I was working on *my* power and presence. People would have to make room for me.

POWER WALK EXERCISE

Pick a crowded street or walkway. Set your intention to create a path for yourself. Feel the power and strength inside your body. Pull up your chest, settle your shoulders. Feel your power centered right below your navel. Begin walking. Take long, comfortable strides. Look straight ahead. Let your arms swing freely at your sides. Feel the energy moving through your body. Feel your presence. Walk with power. Stay loose. Do not adopt a strident, military posture. Move with a sense that you can easily make a path for yourself. Walk purposefully and with vigor.

As you practice this walk on a crowded street, move with so much force and authority that the person coming toward you moves aside. As you walk, say to yourself, "I HAVE POWER. I HAVE PRESENCE." See how many people will move aside for you. See what kind of path you can create for yourself by the sheer force of your intention.

Needless to say, not everyone did. I had several brushes and one crash. But interestingly enough, most people saw me coming and actually moved aside. I feel it. I HAVE POWER. I HAVE PRESENCE."

Change your walk and you not only change how you feel but how people see you.

Body Language

We are talking all the time. Our eyes talk; our faces, hands, and bodies talk. More than half of what we communicate involves physical expression. Dr. Albert Mehrabian's UCLA study showed that 55 percent of our communication value is nonverbal, 38 percent is the voice tone, and only 7 percent is the actual words. In this chapter we're going for the whole enchilada, or at least 93 percent of it.

We read people and make judgments based on our feelings. I always liked the following story of the way this works:

> A criminal trial jury was being selected. A prospective woman juror rose and told the judge she wanted to be excused. The judge asked why, and she stated, "One look at the accused has convinced me that he is guilty." With this, the judge asked her to sit down and be quiet. The person she was pointing to was the district attorney.

How can so much of our communication be nonverbal? Think about it. You and a friend are having a discussion. All of a sudden your friend's vocal pitch elevates, her eyes start to blink rapidly, and her body stiffens. You ask if something you said upset her, and she replies, "I'm not the least bit upset with what you're saying!" Or you're arguing with your boss. Suddenly, his face becomes frozen, he clenches a fist, sets his jaw, and says in a loud and agitated tone, "I'm not angry."

Which do you believe—a person's manner or her words?

We trust the body to tell the truth. Words can lie. Let's see how good you are at reading nonverbal cues. Here's a quiz I designed for our On Camera workshops.

READING PEOPLE QUIZ

Questions:

1. Which is easier to read, the face or the whole body?

2. Which reads in a more positive way, clasped hands or open hands?

3. If someone strokes his chin while he is talking to you, what does this indicate?

4. What is a person saying when her fingers are tapping on the table?

5. If you are talking and a person drops his chin while he is listening or raises his eyebrows, what does this mean?

6. If someone crosses his legs toward you, is this a negative or positive signal?

7. What does shrugging the shoulders indicate?

Answers:

1. It's much easier to read the whole body. People can hide their feelings behind a mask because facial muscles respond easiest to voluntary control. You've seen someone try to plaster on a phony smile to hide his emotion.

2. Open, relaxed hands read more positively. Clasped hands signal guardedness.

3. If someone is stroking his chin, chances are the decision-making process is still going on and he hasn't yet made up his mind. Keep talking.

4. If her fingers are tapping on the table, make your excuses because she just isn't interested in what you're saying.

(continued)

5. If he drops his chin or raises his eyebrows, he questions what you are saying. Now that you know this, use this message to clarify the situation right there. Ask "Do you have any questions?"

6. If he crosses his legs *toward* you, it shows an open attitude. Uncrossed legs or legs crossed toward you indicate a person who is more accessible, more open to communication. If he crosses them away from you, it's a negative signal and shows he is not very open to you.

7. Shrugging either indicates "I don't know" or indifference.

We are reading people all the time.

*What you are not saying is definitely
and clearly communicated.*

We give each other hundreds of clues as to how we feel without saying a word. That's why it's important to get your nonverbal communication to work for you.

GESTURES

Let's get out the video camera again and take a look at your gestures. In many instances, simple awareness is enough to correct a distracting habit.

Speaking creates energy that has to be channeled through your

---

GESTURE CHECK VIDEO EXERCISE

You will need: A video camera
A chair

Instructions: Stand or sit and place your camera so it can see you from the waist up. Start to talk straight into your camera about something you feel passionately about—football, a soap opera, a recent book, your job. Let yourself get comfortable, and tape about five minutes of talk. Let yourself think and talk. Get your opinions out. Now stop the tape. Play it back and watch. Look at your hands and arms. See how you gesture and what gestures you use.

---

physical body. If you have a very slow rhythm and don't use a lot of amplification when you speak, you may not need to gesture. But when most of us get going, the energy of our communication needs to be channeled through our gestures. Let your hands and arms talk as well as your mouth. Most of us either gesture with our arms or, if the energy gets blocked, with our head. You've seen people on television whose hands are tightly locked in their laps while their heads are bobbing like a dashboard doll's.

Distracting Gestures

One of the most distracting gestures I ever witnessed was made by a speaker who kept his hand in his pocket playing with his change the whole time he spoke. Every eye in the audience wandered to his pocket while he absentmindedly jangled away. This is an example of weak, distracting body language. When people are nervous, sometimes they just wind up their arms and let them fly. The problem is that hands and arms busily churning like windmills are not going to empower their communication. Here are five other distracting gestures that can get in the way of your message.

GESTURES: THE FIVE FATAL FLAWS

1. *Pointing fingers* may trigger hostility. It can make people feel picked on. When you do gesture by pointing, keep your fingers together and gesture with an open palm.

2. *Hand-locking*, either behind your body in the royal way or in front of your body in a fig-leaf gesture over your private parts, cuts off your ability to communicate.

3. *Crossing your arms* in front of you signals caution. Use sparingly; it can indicate a closed attitude.

4. *Self-touching* gestures, hands continuously touching your chin, nose, or arm, communicate tension. Scratching is fine. The only exception here are athletes, who may scratch in the wrong place at the wrong time.

5. *Covering your mouth* when you speak halts communication.

Rules of Gesturing

Gestures have to match the style of the people who use them. You can't get away with gestures that are incompatible with your personality. I remember watching President Jimmy Carter give his energy address to the nation using slashing, pounding gestures that were ill timed and misaligned with his style of presentation. His media coaches did him no favor. Here was a soft-spoken man with an almost ministerial presence using empowerment gestures that went against his own natural style. He did something that never works: He gestured for gesture's sake. At a workshop I conducted shortly after this talk, people's comments ranged from "I didn't believe him" to "He pounded the desk at the wrong time." Powerful pounding gestures have to spring from within. They can't be added on for effect. Gestures that are not in harmony with your personality and what you are saying will detract dramatically from your overall message.

THREE RULES OF GOOD GESTURING

Rule 1. Gestures are an asset only when they enhance your natural style. In order for them to work, you must feel them spring from within. Flighty, extraneous gestures don't add anything. They're just a release of nervous energy. True gestures talk. They enhance any communication.

Rule 2. Gestures, in order to be believable, have to match your facial expression, your body posture, and your energy level. We call this "congruency."

Rule 3. Fast gestures tend to blur. The closer you get to another person, the slower the gesture should be.

If you want to learn the importance of congruency, try this exercise:

CONGRUENCY EXERCISE

You will need: Two people
An audience

Instructions: Two people stand up. Person A puts his hands at his side and keeps them there. Person B steps behind him and puts his own hands out.

Now pick a topic. As Person A starts to talk, Person B, behind him, gestures. To the people watching, it is a funny way to learn the importance of gestures matching and being congruent.

Gestures are an important part of your vocabulary. Studies have shown that when full use is made of nonverbal signals, the effect on others is four times greater than it is when words alone are used. Let's look at the way gestures can work for you.

Power Gestures

Powerful gestures are deliberate, smooth, almost orchestrated. You use continuous, unbroken movement that involves the whole body. Confident, self-assured body language indicates that you feel comfortable with yourself and your situation. Assertive gestures give you that extra edge of confidence, but they cannot just be tacked onto what you are saying. They also cannot be premeditated or clash with your words or your personality. They have to be felt, and in order for them to work, they need to spring naturally from within.

POWER MOVES

1. *Starter position.* If you're standing, use your body alignment technique. Move one foot a little ahead of the other foot, and as you communicate lean slightly in toward the other person. Let your hands and arms hang comfortably at your side, or keep them lightly clasped together, waist high, in front of you. Use them to gesture when appropriate. If seated, try the starter position. Put one foot a little ahead of the other while leaning slightly forward with both hands on your knees. You're conveying that you're confident and ready.

2. *Hand out.* When greeting someone, be the first to extend your hand. It's not only welcoming, it's a take-charge signal.

3. *Spread out.* Spreading out is more powerful than keeping your arms close to your body. I remember seeing a picture of Lee Iacocca on his book jacket cover. Both hands were locked behind his head, and he was leaning back in his chair. It's as though he were saying, "Everything is under control." A hands-on-the-hip stance has a similar effect because it reads, "I'm ready for action." Also, when you're straddling a chair, it shows you're ready to take control.

4. *Open hands.* Open hands are preferable to clasped hands. You look ready to communicate. Tightly clasped hands make you read as guarded and may indicate fear.

5. *Steepling.* A gesture that is referred to as "the power gesture" is called the steeple. The fingertips are pressed together (as in prayer) and then separated a few inches with the thumbs still touching. The hands are usually held at about chest level. This gesture signals that you're in control.

(continued)

In the lobby at the Vidal Sasson corporate office is a giant-sized painting of Vidal standing, his hands steepling. When I brought up steepling to him, he told me he had never heard of the steeple. But he sure had heard of power.

6. *Counting.* Another focused, controlled gesture is the counting gesture. It shows you know where you're going. Count by holding one hand out and having your index finger touch the fingers of your other hand. Start with the index finger.

7. *Celebration.* Celebration gestures are big, unifying, and fun. You've seen basketball players giving each other a high five. A politician giving a "V" sign for victory or someone flashing an "O" for okay or giving you a thumbs-up sign are strong unifying power moves.

FACIAL EXPRESSIONS

Let's start by observing ourselves using our facial expressions.

So many people hide their true feelings by wearing a mask. It's easy to hide your feelings this way because facial muscles respond well to voluntary control. Usually we use the facial expression that indicates happiness to hide many of the feelings we don't want people to know about. But some people hide their feelings by wearing a flat, expressionless face. Frozen, inhibited faces just don't work. Imagine a person with a frozen face saying, "I'm having a good time." You don't believe her. Nor do I believe a client who stands at our podium and delivers, flat-faced, the line "I'm excited to talk to you today about . . ." If your face doesn't convey excitement, we don't buy the words. And if you put your face in neutral, you lose a wonderful avenue of communication.

FACIAL EXPRESSION VIDEO EXERCISE

You will need: A video camera
                   A chair

Instructions: Set up your video camera to videotape your-self from the neck up. Focus the camera on your face as you sit in a chair next to a phone.

Turn on the video camera and call a close friend. Ignore the camera, and, as much as possible, have a normal conversa-tion of at least five minutes. When you are finished, rewind the tape and look at your facial expressions. Notice if you are jerking your head up and down or wagging it from side to side. Is your face flat or animated? Do you have any irri-tating habits such as facial grimaces? Do you allow your face to show emotion?

Excitement and animation show in your whole face, especially around your mouth and eyes. Energy communicates through an enlivened face. If your face shows expression, you'll not only com-municate better but your listeners will be drawn into what you are saying. It's very refreshing when someone cracks up with laughter or lets his tears show in public. He cuts through all the hiding in that moment of truth. He connects.

Luckily for us humans, there are some areas of the face we can't control. When you feel really happy or in love, your pupils are go-ing to dilate whether you like it or not. Blushes show through when people are embarrassed. I also like the way some people's eyebrows just take off during a surprise.

Face and Feelings

Research shows that just the expression on your face can influence the way you feel. There is a pattern detector in the brain that reads the emotions your face expresses. What your face expresses, your body feels. People with a "fear face" have an increased heart rate and cooler hands. Anger, sadness, and happiness are all translated from your face to your body. The mouth is where we show happiness and disgust. It's in the eyes that we show joy and fear. Putting on a happy face triggers a genuine emotional reaction in the body. Just arranging your facial muscles to form a smile produces a positive effect on your body. So all those "Have a Nice Day" happy faces are actually reminding us of something very important. You become what you put on your face. If you have a frown on your face, that conveys an unhappy feeling to the brain. A bright look conveys an upbeat message.

Smiles

Should you just plaster an insincere smile on your face? No. Insincerity will not work. Phony "Say cheese" smiles are forced. That's because smiling is not just a matter of moving the facial muscles. Smiling is triggered by emotions generated from thought. *Smiling is an inside job.* If you think of a funny experience you have had, your face will soften, your eyes will have lines around the outer corners, and your smile will come naturally. Remember, smiling happens first in the brain, then on the face.

Can you oversmile? Yes, you can. Particularly if you oversmile in order to appease or gain approval. You need to keep your expression consistent with your message. If you are saying something pleasant, you would naturally smile, but if your message is stern and you accompany it with a smile, you won't be believed.

Ellen was a client whose smiles sprang forth automatically no matter what she seemed to be feeling or saying. She was very nonthreatening with that constant smile, but her problem was that people at work just did not take her seriously. Her insincerity and her insecurity were showing. During a business meeting, because of her discomfort and nervousness, she plastered a weird grin on her face. Her boss was not amused; he called On Camera and made an appointment for Ellen to work with us. We used video feedback to show Ellen how disruptive her smiling was to her overall communication. She learned to smile spontaneously by connecting her smiles to her feelings. Insecure, cutesy smiles are no longer in her repertoire. When Ellen smiles, it's genuine and it doesn't take away her power. It gives her power.

EYE CONTACT

Your eyes are the most expressive part of your body. When you use them well, they shine for you. Let's start with a video exercise to assess your eye power:

EYE CONTACT VIDEO EXERCISE

You will need: A video camera
Two chairs
A friend

Instructions: Invite a friend to talk with you. Sit down and set your video camera so it focuses on your face from the neck up. The video camera needs to watch your face as you have a conversation with a friend. Make sure you do most of the talking about a subject that really makes you think. Politics, education, or your view on population control should work just fine. Tape yourself for at least five minutes. Now, rewind the tape, sit back, and watch your eyes.

After you have watched the tape, answer these questions:

When you are thinking, where do you look: up, down, to the side, or straight ahead?
Are you maintaining eye contact?
Do you frequently break eye contact when speaking?
Do you frequently break eye contact when listening?

Eyes carry power. They are where you read a person's strength or her weakness. Joy and love show in the eyes, as do sadness and anger. Poker players shade their eyes or wear dark glasses because they can't control the expression in them. If they are dealt a royal flush, they are happy and their pupils will dilate or pop. It's for this same reason that someone in love is called "pie-eyed." After all, the most pleasing eyes to look at are twinkling eyes that show warmth and love. Let's take a look at some power eye gestures:

POWER EYE CONTACT

• The first connection you make with someone is through your eyes. You want to make friendly, nonthreatening eye contact using *a gaze instead of a stare.*
• *A stare is a hard look straight into the eyes.* It carries an intensity with it, as if someone is boring his eyes into you. *In a gaze, you look with less intensity at the eyes and focus on the whole face.*

(continued)

POWER EYE CONTACT

• *Maintain* eye contact throughout your conversation, both when speaking and when listening. This is how you connect with people. Look at the whole face, not just the eyes. And maintain as much eye contact as is comfortable. Good eye contact should be fairly constant.

• When searching for an answer to a question, do not look up as if you are hoping for divine intervention or off to the side, which will make you appear shifty-eyed. Train yourself to think without breaking eye contact. *Maintain eye contact as you search for an answer.* It's quite easy to do once you realize you don't need to move your eyes to access information. If you want to break eye contact occasionally, break by looking down.

• *Planting* is a strong eye gesture that President John Kennedy used. When he spoke to someone, he would look from one eye to the other, as though he were planting his message into each eye. What came across to the listener was his sincerity and commitment.

Now that you understand what power eye gestures are, let me tell you about an insurance agent with a serious stare problem. Jean was distraught when she first came to me and said, "I'm in sales, and something's wrong with me. People always say I'm staring at them. They think I'm angry." Her eyes were hard. Intensity shot right through them.

I said, "Jean, in experiments psychologists have been able to get rhesus monkeys to attack just by staring at them. Eyes carry energy. If you look at someone with a critical, nonblinking stare, he will feel as if you are boring holes in him. We need to work with you to soften your eyes so that you *gaze* instead of stare. It will make a world of difference for you." We put Jean on camera and taught her to adjust her eye levels. It didn't take more than two sessions before she had learned to use a friendly, nonthreatening gaze. And what a boon this was to her insurance sales.

Another client, the president of a large transportation company, called me for some confidential work. Jim had recently gotten feedback that his eye contact was poor. He was quite disturbed by this criticism as it came from his company's CEO. Jim walked into the door of On Camera, shook my hand, and made stellar eye contact. He started talking about the feedback he had received, explaining in detail what he hoped to gain from our session. I was wondering where his poor eye contact was. It had been excellent up to this point. I began to talk to him about the logistics of this session, and that's when I noticed he was no longer looking at me. I stopped talking. He looked back at me, and I asked him, "Are you aware that you don't look at me when I talk?" We had taped our conversation, so I was able to show him this very disturbing pattern. He was surprised to see what poor eye contact he made when he didn't have the floor. Continuing our conversation, I explained, "From now on, whenever you break eye contact with me I will stop talking." After a short while, he was able to see how disrespectful it is to look away when someone is speaking to you. He had already mastered half the equation when he came to us: He maintained eye contact and looked at people when *he* was talking. Now he learned to complete the equation and maintain good eye contact while listening to *someone else* talk. If you want to be a strong communicator, it's important to maintain good eye contact whether you are the speaker or the listener.

When you break eye contact, you cut off the communication. Think about it. You're talking to someone and she glances down at her watch. How does it make you feel? As if "time's up," right?

Blinking

Let yourself blink naturally. Unless it's a problem for you, you don't need to think about it. Most of us average about fifteen blinks a minute. People blink more when they're angry or excited. Anxiety can definitely increase your blink rate.

Most politicians have learned to disguise their feelings. President Nixon certainly spoke in a well-controlled manner during the Watergate scandal. His blink rate, however, markedly increased, leading people to feel he might not be telling the truth. When I work with clients with a rapid blink rate, I use the relaxation techniques covered in chapter two to help them settle into a slower, more conscious blink rate.

Now let's look at the Fatal Flaws of eye contact.

EYE CONTACT: FATAL FLAWS

• *Eye dart.* This is when your eyes dart back and forth quickly from side to side. It reads as shifty-eyed and may indicate a person has a fear of what others are thinking about him.

• *Fixed stare.* This happens to a person who is preoccupied. His eyes are set off in the distance, and he is not there. This is a vacant stare.

• *Popped eyes.* This happens when the eyes are opened overwide. It illustrates an intensity, as if a person has been shocked or surprised.

• *Cold, hard stare.* Here is where anger and hostility come through and make the person receiving the eye contact feel uncomfortable.

(continued)

> • *Avoiding eye contact.* You know that averting the eyes does not work when you are speaking or when you are listening. In fact, I've seen studies in which people who maintained good eye contact were rated as more intelligent and more confident than those who didn't.

We've been discussing one-on-one eye contact between two people, but what if you're speaking to a group? I recommend that you find sympathetic eyes, or what someone called "kind eyeballs," and speak first to them. Focus on one person in the audience at a time for at least five seconds. This is called "talking privately." It's easy to connect to one person at a time. If you try to look at everybody at once, you'll get overstimulated. So look in the eyes of various listeners one at a time and your talk will be both relaxed and conversational.

TOUCH

Touch is the most powerful of all the communication channels. It is the language of physical intimacy, and for this reason it is carefully guarded and controlled. Although touch is a gesture of warmth and concern, it can be seen as seductive or intrusive.

Touch also varies in use from culture to culture. I read one study that found that a couple having lunch in San Juan, Puerto Rico, touched 180 times. In Paris, a French couple touched 110 times. A comparable couple in Miami, Florida, touched exactly two times. They touched "hello" and "good-bye." In London, an English duo touched not at all.

Touch comforts in a way no other sense can. It physically and emotionally connects you to another person. A pat on the back, an arm around a shoulder, holding someone's hand can communicate a kind of warmth when words fall short. Some of life's sweetest touches happen when a person takes the hand of or puts her arm around the shoulder of someone who is sad and hurting. The warmth and comfort is palpable.

There are reasons why we want to get in touch. They are referred to as the Touch Truths.

TOUCH TRUTHS

- Studies show that people who are comfortable touching other people have higher self-esteem than those who aren't.
- Research shows that it's harder to say no to someone who makes a request accompanied by a touch. Think about how politicians communicate by glad-handing voters.
- A momentary fleeting touch can establish a positive, temporary bond between strangers, making them more helpful and generous.
- People who shake hands are evaluated as friendlier, warmer, and more sincere than people who do not shake hands.

Expanding Your Touch Comfort Zone

If you're interested in becoming more comfortable with touch, start by using your handshake. You will have many opportunities to reach out and touch somebody's hand. I remember seeing Diana Ross in concert singing a song with the lyrics "Reach out and touch somebody's hand, make this world a better place if you can." She was moving through the audience touching people as she sang about touch. It was a powerful communication.

Experiment by giving someone a pat on the back, or just reach out and hold someone's hand when you want to communicate warmth and affection. Do whatever expands your touch comfort zone and still feels comfortable to you.

If you're involved in competitive sports, hugs and slaps are probably natural to you. Hugs can feel very comforting when they are given between two people—of either sex—who feel close.

But you can also overdo this hugging, touchy-feely business. You don't want to make someone uncomfortable, so touching must be appropriate. I had a Japanese client who was so freaked out by all the hugs she was receiving in California that we designed a hug-blocking technique that allowed her to avoid the hug and substitute a handshake. All you do is shake someone's hand while you straight-arm him and hold him at bay with the other hand. I should have used this technique on myself, as I once created a very uncomfortable situation for one of my clients, an English author. We had had a productive and very rewarding training session, and I enthusiastically reached out and hugged her. Her body stiffened and felt as if it was going to crack into thousands of pieces. At that moment, I realized a handshake would have worked quite nicely.

Personal Space

I had a Brazilian client who liked to get up close into my personal space when he talked. His culture, in general, supports lots of touching and physical closeness. I come from an Anglo background, and I like a fair amount of distance between someone else and me. Like most Americans, I'm comfortable with two to four feet of personal space between another person and me.

Fernando would stand about a foot away and then lean in. When he talked, his hands would reach out and touch me on my arm or shoulder. One time we were standing in my office talking when I realized I had moved backward about three feet and was up against the wall. I could feel him breathing on me. I said, "Fernando, would you please move back so I can peel myself off this wall. I'm feeling very crowded." I knew exactly what had happened; he had violated my personal space. It was amazing how uncomfortable I had become.

The FBI uses an interrogation tactic in which agents totally get in someone's face. They move in and breathe on a suspect in order to get him to crack. People get so freaked out, they confess.

MAKING CONTACT

Let's review some of what we've already discussed and look at the basics of greeting people. When you first meet someone, forget about yourself and focus on him. Make eye contact. Do this by gazing with your eyes at his whole face. Do not just stare, eyeball to eyeball, as this can make people very uncomfortable. If you're wearing sunglasses, take them off.

Smile when you meet, but remember that smiles are an inside job. They have to be genuine. You can't hide behind your smile as a means of self-protection. Forget the phony "Say cheese" smile; we all know the difference between a sincere smile and a forced one.

Shake hands to establish contact. Take every opportunity, even in an informal situation, to shake someone's hand. Give a firm, direct handshake from the elbow; no bone crushing, no fingertips, please. For warmth, use the hand-over-handshake. To do this, lay your left hand over the top of the two shaking hands. Avoid the overzealous pumping handshake and the overly sensuous squeeze.

Say the name of the person you are meeting out loud. Do not just say "Hi, it's nice to meet you." Say "Hi, Jill, it's nice to meet you." This will establish an air of familiarity and put the other person more at ease. If you did not catch her name right then, ask.

Now is the perfect time to correct this: "I'm so glad to meet you, but I didn't hear your name when Francis introduced us." You will find that repeating a person's name helps you remember it. And besides, people like to hear their name spoken.

Remember, focus on the other person. Making him comfortable will assure a good connection. Look at him, shake his hand, smile, say his name. Enjoy the contact!

VOICE

Some people are betrayed by their voices. William, now a star of a television series, leaps to mind. I met him over five years ago when he was modeling and trying to break into acting. Leo, his agent, boasted that his eyes instantly told him if a potential client had that something extra: "If they have it, I can't take my eyes off of them."

Leo brought him to my office. William's long legs were tightly encased in a pair of faded jeans. His broad shoulders bulged under his round-necked Calvin Klein T-shirt. He had long, perfectly cut dark hair, and his clear blue eyes were paled by the tan of his perfectly chiseled face. He was great-looking.

And then he spoke:

"Jesus. I thought we would never get here. Traffic was bumper to bumper all along Wilshire. It took twenty minutes to go one mile." His voice, which was nasal and whiny, clashed completely with his visual presentation. He looked like a hunk, but he sounded like a wimp. His photographs got him interviews for parts, but as soon as he opened his mouth, it was "Don't call us. We'll call you." What surprised me was that he didn't know he was being boycotted by his own voice.

Using some of the voice-assessment exercises offered here, William really listened to himself for the first time and was able to recognize his voice's nasality and whiny tone. Once he saw the problem, we taught him how to increase his breath support and eliminate his nasal twang.

Most actors, unlike William, dedicate a great deal of time to listening to their own voices (often to the exclusion of all others). Most people, however, don't have the slightest idea what they really sound like. I confess that I was already in my early twenties and practicing psychology when I first listened to myself. At the time, I was very conscious that although I had earned my master's degree and was bursting with opinions, people didn't seem to listen when I spoke. Instead, they seemed to dismiss me as a cute blonde.

One day I played back a taped conversation between a friend and myself. Was that high-pitched, breathy voice really mine? Not until I truly listened to myself was I aware of my speaking flaws, which I later corrected by using a tape recorder and voice exercises prescribed to me by a voice coach.

ASSESSMENT EXERCISE: EAVESDROPPING ON YOUR VOICE

You will need: A tape recorder
A friend

Instructions: Tape record a conversation with a friend that lasts five minutes or longer. Have something you need to talk about, and try to forget about the tape recorder and speak naturally. Discuss personal as well as professional matters. When you play back the tape, listen to yourself objectively, as if you were someone else. Then ask a friend to listen with you. Listen with your back to the tape recorder. You'll be more objective that way. Do you hear evidence of any of the following common speaking defects?

In this chapter you are going to listen—really listen—to your own voice. Perhaps you think you already know how you sound. Maybe, for instance, you own a telephone answering machine. Call a friend who has a machine and listen to his taped greeting. Does he sound like the person you know? Probably not. When reading prepared messages, we often speak stiffly, self-consciously. This is not how we sound most of the time.

TEN COMMON SPEAKING DEFECTS

1. Constant interruptions in sound
2. Talking too fast
3. Talking too slowly
4. Nervous, gasping breath
5. Mumbling
6. Nasality
7. Shrillness
8. Inflecting up at the end of most sentences
9. Speaking too loudly or too softly
10. Talking in a monotone

Constant Interruptions in Sound

Constant interruptions in sound such as clearing your throat, smacking your lips, or sucking in your breath are like a glitch in a record. Your voice should be melodious, music to the ears. When you interrupt yourself with unpleasant sounds, you are taking attention away from your message.

A well-known criminal came to our studio before facing the media to promote his autobiography. Here I was, face-to-face with the man who had the notorious reputation of being one of the biggest crooks of our time. It was my job to help him sell the book he hoped would set the record straight. And the first thing I noticed was that although he had an attractive and well-modulated speaking voice, he was constantly interrupting himself by clearing his throat.

The public perception of him was already that of a dishonest man. By continually clearing his throat, he sounded even more suspicious, as if he were fighting his own words. Often, people clear their throats out of nervous habit. But this man had a medical problem. I sent him to a doctor who confirmed, as I had suspected, that he had severe postnasal drip. Medication was prescribed, and he was able to stop clearing his throat and start telling his story. Here is what I recommend to maximize throat comfort:

RECIPE FOR THROAT COMFORT

1. Drink plenty of water.
2. Don't use ice. Cold liquids can constrict your throat muscles.
3. Keep your throat moist with warm lemon water or chamomile tea, which coats the throat.
4. Coffee can give you dry mouth; have water available.

Talking Too Fast

Talking too fast is one of the most common speaking flaws. I hear it most often among bright, lively people. Anna, who trained with me several years ago while making the transition from producer to interviewer, is a case in point. She had grown up in a family that debated hard-news issues nightly at the dinner table. She was skilled at quickly cutting to the heart of an issue. But she was so eager to get her point across that the words raced out of her mouth, falling all over each other. Her rapid speech overwhelmed her listeners. Once she became aware of her problem, she was consciously able to slow down her speech.

Although it's often associated with high intelligence, talking too fast can indicate insecurity. It makes it seem as if the person is afraid people won't hang around long enough to hear what he or she has to say.

Talking Too Slowly

Talking too slowly also has negative connotations. A bore has been defined as someone to whom you ask a question and by the time he finishes answering it, you have forgotten what you asked.

Slow talkers are much less common than fast talkers. Often they are people who choose their words very carefully. And slow talking can be quite effective at the right place and right time; it can help you deliver your message with punch. Flat, slow, monotone voices, on the other hand, will put a listener right to sleep.

Of course, the situation as well as the content determines the desired rate of speech. Recently, I helped a Hughes Aircraft engineer prepare for a press conference in which he would explain why a Hughes satellite wasn't in orbit.

"Am I talking too slowly?" he asked me.

Actually, his rate of speech—about 130 words a minute—was perfect for the technical information he had to impart. If he talked much faster, he would risk confusing people. This slower rate of speech, however, would have been boring if he were trying to fire up enthusiasm for a new satellite launch.

If you look at tapes of Alfred Hitchcock introducing his TV show, you will see and hear that he spoke very slowly . . . to . . . dramatize . . . his . . . words . . . and . . . build . . . suspense. Or watch Robert Preston in *The Music Man*. He spoke very quickly to excite and inspire his audience.

So how do you know if you are talking too fast or too slowly? I thought you would never ask.

ASSESSMENT EXERCISE: TESTING YOUR RATE OF SPEECH

You will need: A book
A stopwatch or a watch with a second hand
A tape recorder
A friend

Instructions: With the help of your friend, time yourself reading aloud for one minute. When the minute has elapsed, mark off where you were in the book. Then go back and count the words. Next, tape record yourself speaking to your friend for one minute. Again, go back and count the words.

Generally, your rate of speech while reading should be between 140 and 160 words a minute. If you read more than 180 words a minute, it may be difficult to understand you. When speaking, I find 170 to 190 words per minute is a good pace.

Nervous, Gasping Breath

Obscene phone callers often have nervous, gasping breath. So did Marilyn Monroe. She used it to communicate sexual excitement. When people get truly excited, sexually or otherwise, they

---

ASSESSMENT EXERCISE: TESTING YOUR BREATH RATE

You will need: A stopwatch or a watch with a second hand
A friend
A book or magazine

Instructions: Give the stopwatch or watch to a friend and stand with a book or magazine open to something you can read aloud.

Ask your friend to call time after one minute, and begin reading aloud and *breathe normally*. Ask your friend to observe your breathing, and count each inhalation and exhalation as one breath—inhale and exhale (1), inhale and exhale (2). Your friend can count silently in his head or mark the time down on a sheet of paper.

Continue reading until one minute has elapsed. Have your friend tell you the number of breaths you took in this minute, then look at this chart:

7 to 11: relaxed, natural breath rhythm
12 to 18: average, possibly shallow and nondiaphragmatic
19 plus: nervous tiny sips of breath without any diaphragmatic breath support

---

begin taking tiny sips of breath, which results in gasping and pant-
ing like a dog in heat. This is fine if you wish to inspire romance
or attract a lot of dogs. It's not helpful when you are about to be
interviewed on television or give a presentation before a group of
people. Most people are afflicted by nervous, gasping breath on
those occasions when they are quite nervous about something. It
happens to many of my clients just as they step before the television cameras. Because they are nervous about being interviewed,
they suddenly start taking small, nervous breaths and gasp when
they speak. It's very important that they correct this breathing pattern because gasping breath makes them sound rushed and insecure. More relaxed breath, on the other hand, makes for a more
confident delivery.

When you listened to your tape-recorded conversation, did your
voice sound rushed, insecure, breathy? Take the breath rate test to
see how fast or slow you are breathing.

Chances are that during this test you automatically slowed
down your breath. You probably are breathing faster in most situations. And the easiest and most important thing you can do to
improve the quality of your voice is to practice the diaphragmatic
and rhythmic breathing exercises outlined in chapter two.

Mumbling

We were training a group of financial planners from a large
savings-and-loan institution to speak publicly. One of the men in
the group spoke clearly most of the time. But whenever he got
down to dollars and cents, he began mumbling:

"I think your best bet would be to invest mumble mumble into
mumble mumble. If you factor in the leveraging, within mumble
mumble, you would realize a profit of mumble mumble mumble."

A man who makes his living helping people plan their financial
future should not mumble when he talks about money. This
financial planner's problem was insecurity at adding up figures in

his head. He wasn't sure enough about what he was saying to speak clearly about money, so we had to work on his verbal command. When you listen to your tape recording, your words should sound distinct. Mumbling is easily detected. Look in the mirror while you are talking. Do your lips move? Most mumblers don't move their lips enough to enunciate properly. Yawn to open your throat. Generally, your lips should move about one finger width apart when you speak. In other words, you should be able to stick your finger in your mouth when talking.

Nasality

Most people with nasal voices, like William the actor, were taught incorrectly to breathe through their nose, and they have to be retrained. A case in point was an unknown actress who, years ago, read for film director Howard Hawks. He told her he wasn't interested in her because of her high nasal voice. She returned to read for him three weeks later with a low, gravelly voice. He was impressed that she had wanted to work so much she was willing to develop a deep, resonant voice. And the rest for Lauren Bacall, as they say, was history.

The only time you should have some nasality is when you say the "n," "m," and "ng" sounds. If you don't open your mouth when you speak, the sound has to come from your nose. The main cause of nasality is a tight jaw, or tension in the muscles in the back of the tongue.

Listen to yourself on the tape recorder once again. Do you sound as if you have a cold? Then you are probably nasal and should practice the following exercises:

CORRECTING NASALITY EXERCISE

• To correct nasality, open your mouth wide enough to get the vowel sounds out. Articulate your words.

• Yawn, stretch your mouth open. Relax your lower jaw and make an "ah" sound while moving it from side to side.

• To get used to hearing the sounds come out of your mouth instead of your nose, hold your palm in front of your mouth and blow into it while saying "Whsssh." Feel your breath coming comfortably out of your mouth.

• Nasal resonance is irritating; you want to use chest resonance, which is pleasing. In order to develop chest resonance, you need to learn to breathe from your diaphragm. Go back and practice the diaphragmatic breathing exercise in chapter two. You should be able to put your hand on your chest, say the words "deep, deep, deep," and feel the vibrations in your chest.

Shrillness

Eavesdrop on yourself during tense situations or moments in which you become excited and enthusiastic. Does your voice take on a high-pitched, highly irritating quality? If it does, you're not alone. If you suspect shrillness, take this test:

ASSESSMENT EXERCISE: TESTING FOR SHRILLNESS

You will need: An audio tape recorder

Instructions: Tape record yourself reading the following statements *with conviction*:

"Get in here, Billy, and clean up this mess! Now. Do you hear me?"
"Oh, I'm so excited to be here. This is the best party I've ever been to."
"It's such a great pleasure to meet you. I can't tell you how much I love your work."
"You mean I got the job?"

Play back the tape recording. Is your voice squeaky and high-pitched? If so read on.

In an attempt to liven up an author who sounded flat, I gave her a few situations in which she would act enthusiastically. As soon as she became enthusiastic, however, her voice became shrill. She is not unusual. Few people are shrill all the time; shrillness comes when we are striving to make a point and are suddenly seized by emotion.

Our bodies are sound-sensitive. That's why shrillness is extremely unpleasant to hear. It produces involuntary muscle tightening just as hearing chalk squealing on a blackboard does. It's a problem more common in females. Men have three pitch patterns; women have four. The extra pitch pattern is squeaky and high. High-pitched voices often rob women of authority and style.

You want to develop a low pitch that is far more empowering than a high squeaky voice.

Shrillness is not difficult to detect. Listen to your taped voice. Do you find it inspires involuntary muscle tightening and constriction of blood vessels? Is it grating and unpleasant to your ears? Do you feel a headache coming on? Shrillness can be corrected by practicing the pitch-lowering exercise that follows.

PITCH LOWERING EXERCISE

You will need: An audio tape recorder
A book
A chair

Instructions: To lower the pitch of your voice, you need to relax your throat. Try this exercise. Sit down in a chair and put a book on the floor between your feet. Relax and let your body slump forward so you are low enough to be able to read the book. In this position audiotape yourself reading in a lowered pitch. Now sit up and read the same passage in a lowered pitch, lowering your voice without bending over. When you play the tape back, you will hear how much lower your voice can sound.

Inflecting Up at the End of Most Sentences

Inflecting up at the end of a sentence means you are unconsciously punctuating everything you say, including assertive statements, with a great big question mark. Inflecting up is fine if you are really asking a question, but it does not enhance statements of fact.

An attorney got dramatic results when she put our voice techniques to use in her own social and professional life. I remember well our first phone conversation.

"Hello? Christen? This is Karen Johnson?"

"It is?" I replied. "Are you sure?"

One of the first things we had to correct was her habit of ending every statement with a question mark. A judge had already told her that her legal presentations lacked conviction. Those question marks caused by inflecting up at the end of sentences were severely hampering her professional performance. Instead of telling the jury that her client was not at the scene of the crime the night of August 23, she sounded as if she were questioning everything she was saying. If she was questioning herself, how could she convince a jury?

Listen carefully to yourself in that taped conversation. If you go up in pitch to make a point, your words will lack authority. Did many of your statements become questions because you inflected up at the end of the sentence? If so, make an effort to begin inflecting down at the end of sentences instead. Lowering pitch and tone at the end of a statement adds strength to your words. Through conscious practice, you can train yourself to remove those disempowering question marks that make you sound insecure.

Speaking Too Loudly or Too Softly

Loud talkers have a reputation for being overbearing, overly aggressive, bossy. Actually, they can be lovely people. I confess that, when swept up with emotion, I become loud. Like my weight, my voice tone is something I must keep under constant surveillance. And self-monitoring is the best antidote.

While helping train Ann, an author and psychotherapist, for her talk-show tour to promote her new book, I noticed her voice was extremely loud. To make Ann aware of her volume, I turned mine up even louder.

"Learning to be natural on television—I don't know if I can do it," Ann would yell.

"Start your rhythmic breathing. It's really quite simple," I would shout back.

Pretty soon we were both screaming. Once she was aware of her volume, she turned it down. Each time she forgot, I spoke even louder to remind her.

Loud voices are much less common than those sweet, shy, itty-bitty voices we can barely hear. Do people constantly request that you speak up? There are times when a soft voice can be very appealing and appropriate, and it does help to drop the volume when you want someone to listen closely. But talking to a group or trying to make an important point to one person aren't those times. In fact, if you speak softly, people won't believe you as much as they will if you project your voice.

If your volume is faulty, you probably already know it. If you speak too loudly or too softly, people have commented.

Do friends often request that you lower your voice on the phone or in public places? Do friends constantly request that you speak up? Do people complain that they can't hear you?

You need to become aware of when to turn up and when to turn down your volume. Master communicators use their voices like the musical instruments they are. If you need to raise your voice, then practice with this voice projection exercise.

VOICE PROJECTION EXERCISE

You will need: A banquet-sized room
A friend

Instructions: Stand with your arms at your sides, and, as you inhale slowly, bring your outstretched arms up over your head until your hands touch. Now open your mouth and exhale slowly, making a voiceless "ha" sound as you slowly lower your arms to your side.

You need physically to get yourself used to speaking with a strong voice. Let's take a powerful word: "Now." Stand in a ballroom or banquet-sized room with a friend five feet away and say "Now" normally. Lean in, project your voice, and say "Now" as your friend stands in the middle of the room. Now really throw your arms and body into "Now" and project it to your friend all the way across the room. Do it until he says he hears you clearly. Continue speaking and projecting your voice to the back of the room. Do not raise the pitch of your voice, just the volume.

Talking in a Monotone

Listen to that taped conversation with a friend one more time. Become aware of your speech pattern. Is it flat and monotonous with no word punch? No emotion? In other words, do you speak with only one tone and no highs or lows to color what you are saying?

Men are the most likely to speak in monotones. The more conscious some men become of their speech, the more monotonous it becomes. They become so frightened of betraying insecurities, they remove all emotion-revealing highs and lows from their voice. Monotones are, of course, the number one killers of political and public speaking careers. Dull monotones do not enhance one's believability or sincerity. Furthermore, monotones are boring. Everything sounds exactly the same.

One of our clients, a minister, was a real intellect and spoke from his head, not from his heart. He read the scriptures in a monotone, flat and uninteresting. Words, to the reverend, were just words, so I prescribed energy pumping and breath support along with word punch techniques. We also used our physical movement coach to loosen up his gestures so he could start adding emotion and physical expression to his sermons.

The word punch assessment is designed to help you decide if you speak in a monotone.

WORD PUNCH ASSESSMENT

You will need: An audio tape recorder

Instructions: Read the following assertive statements into the tape recorder:

1. No, Harold. You cannot have a raise. Furthermore, since you have not lived up to your agreement, I'm going to have to terminate your employment.
2. This report was given to you first, and therefore I'd like you to tell me why it's still not completed.
3. There is something that has been bothering me that needs to be said.
4. That was not my error.
5. I want it now.

(continued)

When you listen to the tape, notice if certain words have punch or pop out. The underlined words in each statement should have been punched.

1. No, Harold. You <u>cannot</u> have a <u>raise</u>. Furthermore, since you have <u>not</u> lived <u>up</u> to your agreement, I'm going to have to <u>terminate</u> your employment.

2. This report was given to you <u>first</u>, and therefore I'd like you to tell me <u>why</u> it's <u>still</u> not completed.

3. There is something that has been <u>bothering</u> me that <u>needs</u> to be said.

4. That was <u>not my error</u>.

5. I want it <u>now</u>.

Read the same authoritative statements into the tape recorder again. This time emphasize the underlined words. Does this second recording seem to have more authority? If so, practice using word punch to break the monotone habit.

Voice Power

Now that you've listened to your voice and detected some of the common speaking flaws, let's take a look at the keys to a *strong* speaking voice.

FIVE KEYS TO A POWER VOICE

1. *Projection.* In order to have the volume you need to project your voice, you must use abdominal breathing for breath support. Use our voice projection exercise.

2. *Tone* is important because it is how we animate our voice. Practice punching words and giving them emphasis. Use our word punch assessment.

3. *Inflection* gives your words meaning. Raising your inflection conveys uncertainty. Lowering your inflection expresses command. Your inflection can reinforce or contradict your words. *Good inflection underlines your message.* Inflect down at the end of sentences to add importance to what you are saying.

4. *Rate* of speech needs to be approximately 180 words per minute. If you talk too fast or too slowly, what you say will go right by your audience. Use the testing your rate of speech exercise.

5. *Articulation.* Open your mouth one finger width when you speak. Pronounce your words clearly. If your words run together, like "didcha wanna," you need to work on the distinctness of the sound of each word.

RAPPORT

Rapport has been called the ultimate power. The reason for this is that it creates a sense of trust, a sense of being on the same wavelength as another person. You get a strong feeling that the other person *understands* you. Psychotherapists refer to this as "joining." When I work with people who are good at building rapport, I tell them they rate high in likability. There are two reasons for this:

1. *They are good at finding similarities between themselves and other people.* People feel responsive toward them because they are able to convey the feeling "I'm just like you." We like people like ourselves.

2. *They are truly interested in another's point of view.* They know how to establish a level of comfort and shared understanding. They may not agree with us, but we feel they hear us and respect our viewpoint.

Likes Attract

Forget about opposites attracting—that's only for magnets. For people, *likes* attract. We like people who are like ourselves. If you want to build rapport with someone (and you do, you do!), you need to show her the ways that you're alike. This happens many times. We find we are talking to someone and suddenly it's "You like to sail!" or "You read murder mysteries!" Even sports or weather can give you a common frame of reference. You're looking for what you have in common because it's very hard to resist your own ideas, your own point of view. So when you find someone else who has the same point of view, it's very attractive. That's why I say it's likes that attract. It's not just the words and ideas, though, because words are such a small part of the communication. If you really want to make someone feel comfortable with you, then listen to *how* she talks. If she speaks softly, or loudly, you can match her volume by dropping, or raising, your voice slightly. And if she speaks very slowly or very quickly, you might even want to speed up or slow down your rate of speech. That makes people even more comfortable. We're often not aware of how we use our voices—therefore, it's very easy to drop into rapport with someone by just slightly adjusting your voice to hers.

Now, if this sounds strange to you, consider people who fall in love. They tend to mirror and match each other's gestures and voice tones. People who are in love engage in an obvious (to the trained eye) mating dance. Without realizing it, they begin to mirror each other's movements. They scratch their arms, reach for their wineglasses, or shift postures rhythmically. When you become intimate with someone, you synchronize or coordinate your speech and gestures with his or hers. This often happens with families and friends in just the same way.

People who are great communicators naturally adjust their rate of speech to get into rapport with another person. They also tend to move as another person moves. When someone smiles, they smile back. If someone sits down to talk and establishes a relaxed body posture, they relax their own posture. If their boss puts her hands on her desk before standing up, they place their hands on their knees and get ready to stand up also. I read an article years ago in one of the weekly newsmagazines about mimicking your way to the top. It pointed out that employees tend to mimic their boss's style of communication. This is not so surprising. When you get into rapport with someone, you naturally face him. Often you adjust your body to match his stance or position.

Imagine you're in a conversation with someone and you face him directly. Only instead of facing you, he angles his body away from yours, turning his shoulder away from you. What has happened? He gave you the cold shoulder. Literally. He's not trying to build a relationship with you.

Now that you understand how to build rapport, you have a choice, and when you like someone, you naturally choose to start to build rapport with him.

Conversational Rhythm

I've got rhythm; you've got rhythm. So do conversations. Think of the earth's rotation . . . soundwaves . . . heartbeats. We are rhythmic creatures. The best conversationalists have great timing, much like jazz musicians who know when to lead into their solos and when to fade out. Good conversationalists know how to interact with people, when to talk and when to listen. When people are comfortable with each other, there is a smooth, rhythmic flow of interaction from moment to moment. People who lack rhythm will often talk too long at one stretch without letting the other person respond.

It is especially important to understand rhythm when you are communicating with someone from another culture or different language background who may throw you off balance verbally by stressing different words or by having different points of emphasis. This can upset the entire conversational rhythm. Even a minute change such as a slight variance in the pause rate between words and statements can cause a disruption in rhythm.

For example, if you are from New York, you may pause for a shorter time after someone else stops talking. You may just jump right back into the conversation. A Californian is often used to longer pauses and may prefer to wait an extra beat before speaking. The result: The New Yorker gets uncomfortable with the longer pause; to her, it is an awkward silence. So she jumps in and starts talking. The Californian feels the New Yorker has interrupted her and is an aggressive person. This can occur among people who share the same language and essentially the same culture just because of a slight difference in pause rate.

Communication is a dance, with both the words and the body language in rhythm. Your body expression and your speech are locked into a beat, and even your eyes blink in synch with your speech.

When you've built rapport with someone, you can feel the rhythm that's been established. There's an ebb and a flow, a synchronicity to a good conversation.

Dress

Clothes do not make the man or woman, but clothing is a potent medium of communication. It carries a lot of information about who you are and who you would like to be. People become more "legitimate" if they are dressed appropriately. Try this: Wear something that doesn't make a statement about you.

Impossible, right? You're *always* sending a message no matter what you wear. And studies show that we come to the aid of people most like ourselves. In other words, if you want to borrow money for a subway ride and you're asking for money from strangers wearing suits, you'll do much better if you're dressed in a suit.

Obviously, our personal appearance plays a very important role in the way people perceive us. During a head-to-toe check, we all make some decisions that affect our judgments and feelings about a person. We need to get from the eyes to the feet to the eyes as quickly and smoothly as possible. Anything that stops the eye and confuses the visual message will act like a glitch in the record and keep us from making a smooth first impression.

The goal of dressing is to choose what makes you feel good and look attractive. All of us need to dress appropriately for our profession. I have coached swamis who looked perfect in saffron robes, doctors and chefs who were only comfortable in their white coats, and porn stars who looked totally themselves in tons of makeup with lots of cleavage.

Clothing should be comfortable so it can move with you. If it upstages you, it's the wrong outfit. One of our clients had a huge success with her first book. She was very much in demand on the talk-show circuit and dressed fashionably and tastefully while on her first tour. But when she came in for training for her second book tour, success had gone not only to her head but to her wardrobe. She came in dressed in an orange taffeta designer dress with an enormous collar and huge shoulders. Her comment was "Isn't this just perfect for *Donahue?*"

My comment was "Just perfect, if you don't mind the dress wearing you."

"What do you mean?" she replied. "I paid $2,500 for this dress. It shows me well."

"It swallows you," I replied.

There was no talking to her. And onto *Donahue* she went, looking like a caricature of herself.

Most of our clients appear in front of the public, so we have an image consultant who helps them with their hair, makeup, and dress. If a rock star needs to fashion an image for his new music video or if Betty Crocker wants its spokeswoman updated, that's a simple job for us. The hard cases are the people who come to us and resist image consultation.

When a rap star comes in during a ninety-degree heat wave wearing a ski cap and parka, takes off the ski cap, and has cellophane wrap all over his head, we don't say a word. This is "the look." But I remember one woman who was going on the talkshow circuit to promote a product. She came in looking as if she had been pulled through a hedge. Her hair was mangled, her clothes disheveled. Even her outfit was jarring. She looked as if she figured if she wore enough color, something was bound to match. This woman was not aware of the visual impression she was making. Our image consultant went to town with her.

Color

When you choose colors, you need to pick not only what is flattering to you but colors you find uplifting.

Dark colors like black or dark blue are thought to make a person look more dominant. That's why, in presidential debates, the candidates usually wear dark suits. They're trying to look powerful. But oftentimes the suits are so dark they read as black and funereal. Red and orange put you in the foreground, and men and women are often advised to wear a dark blue suit with a bright red tie or blouse. This is considered a *power outfit*. But you already know that power comes from the inside and no tie or suit is going to give it to you. Clothing can *add* to your power, but it can't *provide* power.

Studies show that blue is rated as the most pleasing color, gray as the least pleasing. At On Camera, we prefer our clients wear colors that flatter them and that they feel comfortable in. It can't be said too often: It's not what you wear on the outside as much as what you project from the inside that characterizes true self-power.

CHAPTER FIVE

WORDS CAN EITHER WOUND OR HEAL

I only get in trouble when I talk.
—Anonymous

As you develop your outer Star Quality, you will find it's easier to express yourself and to get your thoughts and feelings out. You will also learn to edit what you say, but you won't always get it right.

Often the best you can do is find humor in the dumb things you're occasionally bound to say. A woman was introducing a well-known speaker to the audience. She gave a long introduction filled with praise. Then she said, "Now may I present . . ." No name came. Her memory was blank. She turned to the speaker, smiled, and asked, "What *is* your name, anyway?" The audience erupted into laughter. Contrast this situation with that of the senator who was talking to the Senate about "orgasms found in municipal water throughout the country." When he was greeted with uproarious laughter, he realized he should have been talking about "organisms" and rushed from the room red-faced. It all comes down to attitude.

Words can be used to instruct, arouse, and heal—or you can use them to shoot yourself or someone else in the foot. Verbal communication can be very powerful—two people communing, speaking, connecting to each other—or it can be as painful as two people attacking and abusing each other.

Talk can be words rushing aimlessly out of your mouth, disconnected and meaningless, or it can be deeply connected to your truth. You can speak from your heart and touch people with your thoughts, words, and ideas, or you can just open your mouth and blab on and on, sounding like the drone of a one-note samba.

We should honor our words and value our speech because words have the power to wound or to heal.

SPONTANEOUS TALK

As adults we learn to edit out our baser emotions—but too many times we edit ourselves so tightly that we don't express our true feelings. The freshest talk is spontaneous talk. That's why comedians are interesting conversationalists. They're willing to have fun, take risks, let it fly. The most creative comedians are totally in the moment . . . reacting, ripping, developing material, and entertaining their listeners. The point is:

When you talk about your feelings, conversations come alive.

Small talk is important to break the ice with strangers. It is the opening volley—whether the subject is sports, weather, a current event, whatever—that starts the conversation. But without passion or emotion, all conversation becomes small talk.

If you tell your story without connecting to your feelings, you become an empty talking head. But when you make that connection, you allow yourself to communicate from your essence. You learn to go deep, to draw on your feelings, to speak from your heart. Then you experience the uplift that comes from great conversation. When you speak your truth and touch people with your words, it is exhilarating.

FEELING TALK

A good example of public feeling talk occurs when Tom Hanks wins an Oscar. His acceptance speeches are filled with feeling. When he starts to tear up and talk about "the woman who I share my life with, who has taught me and who demonstrates for me every day just what love is," his vulnerability fills the screen. You'd have to have a heart of stone not to be touched by his emotion-filled words.

So much of the alienation and loneliness we experience today is a result of our emotionally blocking off our communication. It is painful to talk *only* on a superficial level. It hurts when you're with people and you don't feel open or connected to them. That's what makes taking the risk of putting your thoughts and feelings out worth it. You have a chance to touch and be touched by another person. You have opportunities to feel moved, connected . . . to be heard, to commune with another.

Our feelings are an important part of this experience. They allow us to speak from our truest place—whether that place is fear, anger, inspiration, or joy. Our thoughts are different from our feelings, so if we stay only in our head trying to figure things out, we will lack a deeper emotional connection to our words. They're just words—disconnected and devoid of feeling. This is dishonest communication.

True communication involves *all* of you. Your head and your heart are engaged. You stay interested because you're taking risks. You're supporting yourself by telling your truth. Your feelings show you what needs to be said. If you feel anger or uneasiness, state that. This was a hard lesson for me to learn because I wanted so much to fit in and be liked. But no one can fit in all the time or be liked by everyone. It's much better to be true to yourself and speak the truth.

JUST SAY IT EXERCISE

You will need: A friend
A watch

This exercise can be done alone, but it's better with another person.

Instructions: Stand and face your friend. Pick something controversial that you feel passionately about. Start talking. Say anything that comes into your head. Talk quickly. Don't stop talking. Speak loudly. Get those words out. Lose your self-consciousness. Let those words flow. At the end of one minute, stop.

Discuss your feelings with your friend.
Did you feel comfortable talking nonstop?
Were you surprised you could think of things to say?
How did it feel to speak loudly?

Make adjustments and try it again. Look at your friend and speak passionately for one minute. Don't edit, just let the words fly. Use this exercise to loosen yourself up so you can speak freely and say what you want to say. Now, it's your friend's turn.

Self-confidence is a big component of being a good communicator. You have to trust yourself, expose your feelings, take risks if a conversation is to come alive. It's a curse to be so self-critical that you edit yourself down to the word, always feeling afraid you'll say the wrong thing. It's just as big a problem if you go out of your way to try to figure out what someone else wants to hear and then massage her with insincere flattery.

It takes courage to say what you feel. To let someone know when you feel attacked or slighted. To make strong statements. To risk disapproval.

Some of our clients need to learn to speak freely about what concerns them. They hold back even when they have something important to say. In order to free them up to communicate easily, we use an exercise that allows them to get attention for themselves as well as for what they want to say.

TRUTH TALK

It takes self-trust to look someone in the eyes, stay open to your feelings, and then express those feelings freely. This can lead you to have a rich, rewarding communication that can move you to a place of deep fulfillment.

My grandmother once told me she never regretted the things she did, only the things she didn't do. For me, it's the same with truth. I don't have regrets when I speak my truth. My only regrets come when I don't speak my truth. The story of the Italian woman who was singing an aria in a hall in Bologna is an example of learning truth talk. She was singing off-key and having great trouble with the piece. A bystander wandered in, heard her singing the same lines over and over, and asked what was happening. Her teacher replied, "She is singing until she gets all the bad notes out." You learn to speak the truth like this woman learned to sing. This might sound a little strange until you find the cour-

---

TRUTH TALK EXERCISE

You will need: A friend
Two chairs

Instructions: Pick a friend, someone you feel close to. Sit down facing each other. Slow down your speech and speak as accurately as you can about some experience that was difficult for you. It should be something you have never told your friend. Tell her what feels totally true to you. If you find yourself changing things, trying to rewrite the past, stop and see if you can honestly speak what is in your heart.

Ask your friend to tell you what she heard. Is this what you meant to say? How do you feel? Do you feel open or closed? Do you feel a sense of relief at having spoken from your heart? Do you feel more alive?

---

age to speak with clear intention and feeling. But as you learn to speak your truth passionately from the heart, it is beautiful—like great singing.

TRUTH TROUBLE

Truth can be a gentle sharing, or it can be used as a weapon to attack and wound.

Rhonda was an acting teacher who liked to yell. She defined herself by intimidating people and trying to get power over them. Her students were the perfect prey. After all, we were paying her to learn to act. Her assessments of us were often accurate . . . and cruel. She would just attack. One of us would ask a very innocent question and Rhonda would spring into action saying, "What I want to know is, how does he feed himself? Behind that dumb exterior lies a fool." We would squirm or laugh uncomfortably when she ripped someone. This woman was brutal. But ultimately powerless. Her brutality was not honest. It was just part of her act.

One of our clients, Phyllis, was not brutal but certainly a little straightforward with the truth. As she got good at telling her truth, she got just as good at telling you yours. She was quickly switching from "my truth" to "your truth" and started telling people exactly what to do in the name of truth.

We showed Phyllis how to start asking questions. She didn't have to force her ideas on anyone. She could use a question instead. She no longer said, "Your hair looks awful" or "You can't wear purple." She eased into her truth by saying, "Do you like your hair when you wear it shorter?" or "What about lilac, would that be a good color on you?" Of course, if anyone asked Phyllis her opinion, she would gladly give it.

SIX TALK TACTICS

There are several techniques that will strengthen your Star Quality and improve your communication skills. I call them Talk Tactics. They are:

1. Alignment techniques
2. Positive language patterns
3. Undertalking—less is more
4. Pink elephants
5. Interruption techniques
6. "I" versus "You" messages

Alignment Techniques

When discussing an issue, it's important to agree before you disagree. Start by finding a topic on which you both agree, as this allows the person to whom you are speaking to listen with an open mind. This technique was brilliantly demonstrated in 1962 by Attorney General Robert Kennedy, who had the difficult task of enforcing school integration in Alabama. This was a very unwelcome idea in most parts of the South. Kennedy knew it would be hard to interest people in the concept of integration, so he didn't even try. He started talking about law and order and our commitment as Americans to uphold the laws of the land. Only after he got agreement on law and order did he introduce school integration. This is how alignment techniques work. You start by finding an area of agreement. After that, you open the door to new possibilities.

As one of my clients observed, "Saying 'You are absolutely wrong' makes no sense anymore. These are 'fightin' words.' " It is easier to say something inclusive like "I respect the intensity of your feelings, and I'd like you to hear my thoughts on this" or "It appears to me . . ." Or even "That's an interesting idea, but here's another way of looking at it."

When you're in alignment, there is a gentleness that allows you to use healing rather than hurting words. You don't jump in saying "Don't do this" or "Do this." Rather than barking orders, you ask respectfully, "What do you think of this? Do you think this would work?"

You also learn that if you need to criticize or correct someone, you can do it constructively. Alice Roosevelt Longworth's comment "If you have nothing good to say about anyone, sit down here next to me" is wickedly funny. But there's a big difference between joking about yourself or a public figure and personally attacking someone.

Correcting or criticizing needs to be done sensitively because no one likes to be shown up as wrong. It's very easy to take cheap shots. I remember a group training session for some hardened advertising executives who took no prisoners. After the first presentation, one of the admen spoke up, "That sounds like shit, Al."

"Who the hell are you talking to?" Al shot back.

"To this bag of Doritos, airhead," came the reply.

I could see we were in trouble. The hostility level was in the red zone. The group members had no idea how to correct or influence each other. They were totally into making each other wrong.

When you're correcting someone, you have to leave him a way out. It doesn't work to make people wrong or attack them personally. Start with something they're doing right, and then make a gentle correction. If the adman had said, "Your examples are good, Al, but I don't understand the focus," he would have greatly increased his chances of getting a rational reply.

Positive Language Patterns

You can be *against anything* or *for something*. There's a world of difference between these two concepts. What you are against works against *you*. You fight it. Your energy goes into opposing. When you're *for* something, you shift to supporting and improving it.

The idea is going from the "don't" to the "do." One of our communication trainers, Ron, always uses this example: "Do you hate being late?" or "Do you love being on time?" Each statement creates an entirely different feeling in the body. When you say, "I hate being late," you are fighting what is happening and you create an upset feeling inside you. Try saying "I love being on time." If you find yourself getting stuck correcting someone by saying "I hate it when . . ." try switching to "Wouldn't it be better if . . . ?"

What happens is you shift from a negative to a positive. When you get rid of the don'ts—

"Don't be late" translates to "Please be on time."

"Don't forget" changes to "Please remember."

—you're no longer creating a negative expectation. You're creating a positive one.

Just look at the difference between saying *"Why can't you?"* and saying *"What if we?"*

"Why can't you?" is accusatory. "What if we?" suggests there may be a way to work together to improve the situation.

Pay attention to the words you choose. You get too emotionally plugged in when you say, "I'm really furious" or "I'm ballistic." Those strong words affect your nervous system. Tone them down to something like "It annoys me" or "I get concerned when . . ." Edit yourself. When you hear yourself saying "I hate . . . ," try "I don't like . . ." Don't get yourself all riled up by saying "I'm really worried." Soften it with "I'm concerned." Lower the intensity, and defuse the charge.

The only time you want to increase the intensity of your words is when you're speaking about positive emotions. In describing how you feel, you can use the words "good" or "fine" or you can up the intensity and use "perfect" or "fabulous." Not only will you be choosing more powerful words, you will be using words that affect your nervous system positively.

Compliments have a positive effect on ourselves and others. I once read a study that said children get four times as many criticisms as compliments. That could be why, as adults, we respond so well to praise. We're starved for it. *Vogue* editor Diana Vreeland was aware of this problem when she commented, "My God! If you think someone is attractive, you must say, 'I think you're awfully attractive.' We've absolutely got to build ourselves up." She was absolutely right. Besides, it's a lot easier to make a change if we first hear what we are doing right before we hear what we are doing wrong.

Sincere compliments have a positive effect on you because they reflect concern and caring. Just hearing that someone noticed a change in you, no matter how small, is affirming.

Patience is not my long suit. I had been standing at a bank tell-er's counter for some time while he searched for a supervisor who could approve my transaction. I was starting to shuffle, groan, and generally work myself into a hissy fit when the teller came over and said, "Thank you for your patience." I was about to explain that I wasn't patient at all. But something shifted. I felt the effect of his compliment and calmed down. It amazed me that even an undeserved compliment worked.

Undertalking—Less Is More

If you want to be convincing, be brief. We use too many words. Most of us talk not only too long but too much. The convincing person gets to the point quickly.

Overtalking is the biggest problem we have with our clients. If you come to get prepared for the talk-show circuit, then the first thing we do is help you identify your key messages, or "talking points." Once we know what you want to say, then we help you get "bite-sized," so you can speak concisely in what are called tele-vision sound bites. When I started On Camera in 1978, we talked about information imparted on television as being in twenty-to-thirty-second sound bites. Today, that is long. We currently coach people for eight-to-twelve-second sound bites. Learning to talk bite-sized is very helpful as you train yourself to state your message quickly. You don't have time to back into your information—on TV or in real life. If you learn to think in "headlines," you can easily billboard what you want to say.

One of our clients, an actor, was being hounded by the press because he had recently been involved in a two-car collision in which one of his passengers had been seriously hurt. Rumors were flying that he had been drunk the night of the accident. He was about to go on a talk-show tour to promote his new movie, and his agent called and asked us to help Chet focus on answering ques-tions about the accident and stress that he was being maligned by the press and had not been charged with drunk driving. When we saw Chet and questioned him, he had a long story: "I was out with two of my friends. We were playing cards. I had two beers the whole night. We watched a movie. It was two and a half hours later that I drove. My blood alcohol test was negative. The truth is I was stone sober. The only problem is I was on the car phone talking to my girlfriend, and I may have missed something. I don't really know." This was in saga form, not sound bite. He only needed one sentence. When asked if he was drinking at the time of the accident, he needed to answer, "No. My blood test was negative." After you give the headline, then you can fill in the details, but you must put the positive information up front where it belongs.

I have described several coaching tips for a very time-sensitive medium: Television time is expensive. But that's exactly how we should treat our *own* time—as an expensive commodity. This way, when you hear yourself rambling, you will stop, edit yourself, and move to the bottom line.

We've all been in social situations in which someone has your ear and can't let go. She is talking about the kids, dogs, her surgery—anything. Your eyes glaze over as you wonder if she will ever get to the point. Here is a person who has never learned to "self-edit."

It's even worse in a business meeting when one executive drones on, repeating the same information four different times, adding extraneous details, needlessly embellishing his report. Finally, you hear a frustrated associate shout, "What's the bottom line, Bill?" and someone else chimes in, "Just cut to the chase."

It's the responsibility of each of us to keep our information bite-sized—to edit ourselves and to headline by putting the most important information up front where it belongs.

Most communication problems occur when someone has finished what he wants to say but keeps on talking . . . and talking . . . and talking . . . and talking. . . .

Pink Elephants

Many times, what's *not* being said is more important than what is being said. When something is occurring but not being acknowledged, it is called a pink elephant.

One of our clients, a cruise line, had scheduled four days of communication training at On Camera. Just days before the start of these trainings, the cruise line was acquired by a large multinational corporation. The first group of sales representatives came into our seminar in a very agitated state. It seems they were conducting selling seminars regularly and corporate headquarters had advised them not to discuss the acquisition. Right. Here was this big pink elephant sitting in the middle of the room, but everyone was just supposed to ignore it. These salespeople were making presentations to hundreds of people and talking about their ships. You can imagine the questions they were asked: "What is the name of the new company?" "Will you have the same cruises?" "Will my tickets be honored?"

We phoned the vice president of sales and explained that his salespeople needed to learn how to speak about the acquisition. The first thing we did was show them how to bring up and use this underlying pink-elephant issue in order to clear people's minds. We suggested reassuring statements about the old tickets being honored. We even suggested using humor for some issues. By the end of our session, we had shown the sales representatives that they couldn't possibly avoid the pink elephant. He's too huge and loud, and he sits right in the middle of the room just waiting to be acknowledged.

Of course, sometimes the elephant does have to be sidestepped, if not ignored. An author came to us with a pink-elephant problem that was threatening to interfere with her book tour. She was a well-known author who had written a salacious novel. Her publisher was concerned that because Karen had a reputation as a bisexual, this issue could become the focus of her media tour.

"What is your sexuality?" had become a threatening question, and Karen overreacted every time she was asked. "None of your business," she would respond defensively. Karen was overreacting because although in the past she had publicly talked about her bisexuality, she did not want this personal issue to pull focus from her sure-to-be-best-selling novel.

Karen learned that it was okay not to discuss her sexual orientation on national television. "This is a novel about sex, not about *my* sex life," she would say. This is one pink elephant that was not invited into the room.

But, in general, when you notice yourself dancing around a delicate issue, bring it out into the open, where it can be addressed. There's a lot of power that comes when you stop trying to ignore or hide something and just bring it out into the light.

The best recent example of this came right before the 1992 presidential election. The question of Bill Clinton's extramarital affair was threatening to overwhelm his campaign. Instead of ignoring or denying the problem, Clinton went on *60 Minutes* and said he and his wife had had problems in their marriage but that they'd worked them out and they were in the past. Without specifically acknowledging an affair, the president-to-be implied that he'd done certain things but that they were private and no longer relevant. And it worked. At least it worked well enough so he won the election.

Interruption Techniques

What people say is not necessarily what they mean. Ask questions. Get involved. Find out what is *really* meant. Interrupt when you need to clarify an issue. Interrupt when you see a conversation wandering or expanding out of control. Ted Koppel is someone I consider to be the "king of interruption." Because his show, *Nightline,* is broadcast live, he has learned to listen carefully and edit on-air. Koppel interrupts a guest who is being repetitious or dodging questions, and he has no trouble demanding, "Let me ask the question."

You don't have to be a television interviewer to understand that the smoothest way to interrupt is by using agreement. If you agree with what someone is saying, just interrupt with "Exactly" or "Yes," and begin your comments. This can be done very politely. If this doesn't work or you don't agree with what the person is saying, raise your voice slightly, lean in, and in an agreeable tone say, "Excuse me." Now if this person still has not let you into the conversation, you have to ask yourself why you're continuing to listen to a monologue. Use an even heavier voice tone. Put some irritation in it and say, "Would you be willing to let me finish my statement before you start yours?" or "Would you be willing to complete your statement so I can start mine?!"

You have a responsibility for the quality of your conversations. Your input is important, and when the conversation is no longer interesting to you, you need to move on.

"I" Versus "You" Messages

"You did it." "You started it." "You don't know what you're doing." If you're talking, you're in trouble. Why? Because you're focusing on someone else's behavior.

Use "I" messages to speak about your own thoughts and feelings. By taking responsibility for your feelings, your communication is more direct.

Here's how this works:

"You did it" becomes "I'm not sure I would have done it that way."

"You started it" becomes "I probably would have called first."

"You don't know what you're doing" becomes "I also had trouble figuring out what to do here."

Talking to a person in a judgmental way weakens communication. Blaming tries to point the finger at someone else. Say how you feel. It's far more powerful to share from your own point of view. That's why "I" messages are a lot stronger than "you" messages.

THE FATAL FLAWS

Talk should be empowering. It gets disempowered when you use weak words, qualifiers, and nonwords. It really goes south when you start complaining. Here are the four fatal flaws:

1. "Should" and "trying"
2. Hedging and qualifying
3. Nonwords
4. Complaining

"Should" and "Trying"

"Should" and "trying" are weak, disempowering words. They rob you of authority. Forget about what you *should* do. Think about what you *will* do. "Should" gets in the way of doing.

"Trying" is even worse. "Trying" is not doing. "Trying" is an excuse. "I *tried* to do it." "I really *tried*." You don't try to do something. You either do it, or you don't. Listen to the difference. Say "I *tried* to do it." Now say "I did it" or "I *am* doing it." Big difference.

Hedging and Qualifying

Another way to disempower your communication is to use words that hedge or qualify what you say. When you say, "I'm not sure, but . . ." it turns what you are saying into a weak statement. If you want to further weaken your case, state, "It's only my opinion." The phrases "Don't you think?" "Shouldn't I?" and "Isn't it so?"

undermine what you just said and make you sound unsure. Adding a qualifying phrase like "Correct me if I'm wrong" at the end of a statement begs for disagreement. Make strong declarative statements, then you won't qualify or weaken your remarks. "I want your report by 3:00 P.M., Bill" is a lot stronger than "I'm not sure, but isn't your report due soon?"

Nonwords

Most people use "umm" and "ahh" to insure that they won't be interrupted. It's a way of holding on to the conversation. "Umms" and "ahhs" show your fear of being interrupted and call attention to the fact that you are now searching your mind for what you want to say next. Try silence; whenever you hear yourself start to use a nonword, pause, collect your thoughts, and then continue on. Thoughtful pauses will make you sound more intelligent and confident than "umms" and "ahhs."

One of our clients, Dr. Shaw, was the head of a large electronics firm. He was a strong presenter, but he had one verbal flaw—he constantly interrupted himself with ahhs, uhhs, and other nonwords. In any situation, constant use of nonwords will cause you to seem unsure of what you are saying and detract from a powerful image.

Shaw started his speech by saying, "In the, ahh, seventeenth century, umm . . . it may have been . . . ahh . . ." We taught him to replace those nonwords with silence, or what I call creative pauses. Used effectively, these pauses add great impact to your verbal message. While collecting your thoughts about what to say next, it's best to say nothing at all.

To get rid of "umms" and "ahhs," listen to yourself talk so that you become conscious of these nonwords. Awareness will help them drop away.

Poor word choices and using nonwords are communication flaws that with awareness you can easily correct.

ELIMINATING NONWORDS EXERCISE

You will need: An audio tape recorder

Instructions: Start taping. Now make a statement and stick an "umm" or an "ahh" in. Make the same statement, but where you "ummed," pause instead. Play the tape back, and listen to yourself. Notice how the "umms" and "ahhs" pull focus from what you are saying. To correct your normal conversational flow, all it takes is the willingness to listen to yourself talk and when you add an "umm" or "ahh," stop and replace it with a pause. Use the tape recorder to increase your awareness. Monitor your conversations, and you will remove these distracting fillers by adding a creative pause.

Complaining

Writer Jane Wagner says, "I personally think we developed language because of our deep inner need to complain." The truth is that when people talk, they refer to unpleasant emotions twice as often as pleasant emotions. You hear "I'm in a bad mood" a lot more than you hear "I'm in a good mood."

Complaining, whining, and griping all take us to a very unsatisfying place where nothing is right. You look for things that are wrong. Once you get stuck in this complaining place, your energy drops. You start finding fault with everything. I've been there, and it's no picnic.

The problem with complaining is that you're focusing on what's wrong, on the negative, the no, and it pulls you to a place of dissatisfaction. Move out of the complaint as quickly as you can. It's like tar; you can easily get stuck in it. The solution is to make a request. Instead of "I can't stand it when you leave the door to my room open. You always do that. I can't believe how selfish you are. How many times do I have to ask you?" you could say, "Please close the door." Make your request specific, and keep it brief.

I have seen people in personal relationships get into a complaining rut. Sue was in the habit of complaining about the man she lived with. "I listen to him, but he never listens to me." When we suggested she stop complaining and make a request, her response was "I couldn't say anything. I wouldn't want to hurt him." When we suggested that her needs and feelings were just as important as his, she agreed to talk to him. Later Sue called us excitedly to report, "I did it. I talked to him and requested that he give me more of a chance to talk. He had no idea he hadn't been doing this." Six months later, Sue reported, "He still interrupts me from time to time, but as soon as I point this out to him, he apologizes. It wasn't such a big deal after all." The moral of the story: If you hear yourself complaining, stop and make a request.

POWER TALK

In *Women Who Run with the Wolves*, Clarissa Pinkola Estes speaks of a woman whose "main source of power is speaking candidly on her own behalf." I like that. Speaking your truth, telling your feelings, being yourself—that's power. If you close your eyes to the things you don't like and passively accept the people around you who hurt you, you shut down. Your instincts shut down. You don't react to things correctly. You give away your power.

Much of the time we speak in a reactive state. We're responding to something that has already happened. What is empowering is generative speaking, which happens when we speak from our creativity about what is important to us. When you speak passionately and are deeply connected to what you are saying, not only are you speaking with power but you are getting nourishment from what you say. Think about Martin Luther King, Jr., and his "I Have a Dream" speech. It was a powerful speech. He inspired us by painting word pictures. The passion, the enthusiasm, the commitment were all there.

Power talk isn't always inspirational, but it has a force that can't be ignored. Take Ann, for example.

Talking and Selling

Ann is an advertising executive. Her company sent her to On Camera to participate in a training program for presentation skills. When she got on her feet to begin her presentation, we noticed her voice was squeaky and she was racing through her words. You got the feeling she was thinking, "I've got to show them, convince them, wring their necks." If she had worked any harder, she'd probably have had an aneurysm right on the spot. The problem with Ann, like a lot of executive women, is that she was trying too hard. The minute she stopped talking, she felt she had lost control. She did not trust herself. Her head was bobbing rapidly up and down, and her smile seemed pasted on. She needed to slow her rate of speech, strengthen her voice tone, and add some strong gestures.

"Let's take a look at the video," I said. She seemed relieved to have stopped. The playback was sheer torture for Ann. "I look like I'm begging for business! I'm so insecure."

"Let's cut to the chase," I told her. "What do you charge?"

"Our retainer is ten thousand dollars a month."

"How can you possibly justify that kind of fee?"

Ann dropped her eyes. "I don't know."

"That's your insecurity talking, Ann."

"But we're so small here; there are only three of us in our department," she pleaded.

"Wait a minute, Ann. This sounds like a reverse sell."

Changing my tone, I leaned in and glared. "Tell me what you can deliver that nobody else can."

She paused, locked eyes with me, cocked her head, and shouted, "More bang for your buck!"

Everyone laughed. The room was alive again. She told me, "I've worked at those big agencies with lots of firepower, and you know what? Three quarters of the work gets lost in the paper shuffle between offices." She was using powerful, deliberate gestures. "With us, it's simple: We deliver." What had changed was that she was no longer asking. She was telling and selling with confidence! There was no arguing with her. She had shifted her attitude. Her voice was slower, her gestures stronger. Ann had learned the first principal of sales: You must sell yourself before you can sell anyone else.

I asked her again, "What do you charge?"

Again she paused, leaned in, locked eyes with me. "Ten thousand dollars a month. That's a flat fee. All expenses are add-ons." She had found her power, and $10,000 hardly seemed enough.

Attitude defines how well you sell your point of view. For example, in the middle of the Depression, the New York Yankees asked Babe Ruth to take a salary cut. When he held out for his $80,000 contract, the club owner asked, "Why should you be paid more money than the President of the United States?" Ruth replied, "I had a better year."

Social Workers and Engineers

You are talking, working to get a positive response, but it's not happening. You realize your words are falling flat. Even worse, they seem to be falling on deaf ears.

What's the problem? The problem is everyone you talk to is not like you. People hear your words through their own communication filters. You may be working hard to reach them, but you're not successful because you're not speaking their language.

It's not so much what you're saying but how your audience receives your communication that's important.

★★

When you're talking to a friend, you have a good chance of being understood because you know him. His values, beliefs, and thinking style are not foreign to you. You know how much he does or doesn't enjoy humor, how technical your descriptions need to be, and whether to take the time to socialize or move right to the point. You understand the communication style, so it's easier to communicate.

But what if you're talking to a group of people you don't know? If you want to appeal to the widest cross section of people, your communication needs to be task-oriented *and* people-oriented. This is how it works:

Imagine you're speaking to an audience of two very different types of people. Half the audience is made up of very task-oriented engineers. The other half is made up of people-oriented social workers. You need to deliver a balanced communication. How?

When speaking to the engineers, you need to present technical information in an organized way. You know that technically oriented people—like engineers or accountants—like facts, figures, and details presented clearly.

The social workers, you realize, are more interested in people and relationships. You understand that people-oriented persons—like psychologists or social workers—enjoy a more personal approach to conversation. They are interested in people's feelings and are comfortable discussing relationships among people.

Tailor your talk to include these two divergent groups—the engineers and the social workers. This way you will concentrate on people issues, while you also solve problems and present your information in a clear and thorough way. To make sure the greatest number of people receive your information, be sure to tell people-oriented stories and anecdotes while building a case and backing up your information with facts and figures. You will be both task-oriented and people-oriented in your conversation and will have a greater chance of reaching the largest group of people.

Talking Publicly

John wanted to learn how to talk with force to a large audience. He had already done his preparation and knew his material. It is not high art, however, to plan everything you want to say, write it down, and then get up and read it. Doing this locks you into an artificial-sounding, overcontrolled place in which you have little room for warmth or inspiration. The rule here is exactly what former British Prime Minister Harold MacMillan said: "Know exactly what you want to say—have no idea how you're going to say it."

Great communication takes place "in the moment." It isn't artificially wrapped up weeks before. It happens in the here and now. If you're giving a talk or speech, it's good to start by writing out your ideas to get them in order. Then reduce your speech to specific points and let yourself talk conversationally to your audience.

The process of learning to talk in public is very simple. Let me show you how it worked with John, who started out being dangerously boring.

John was a young man who represented an asbestos-removal company. He asked if I would look at a videotape of a recent speech he had made. Viewing the tape, I saw John making a speech to about two hundred people in a large, dimly lit room. Glasses were clinking, tableware was clanging. As people carved their chickens, there was little to distract them from their dinner. John seemed to be on remote control and looked as if he had fallen asleep at the podium. His eyes were downcast, glued to his paper. His voice was flat, his arms were limp.

I invited John to come to my office. He said, "I realize I'm not holding my audience."

"Let's get this into perspective, John. Your audience is comatose. The room is dark; your slides are boring, they're filled with far too many words; your speech lacks focus; your delivery lacks enthusiasm. The only time you managed to grab their attention was when you told them they were releasing a substantial amount of asbestos each time they put on their brakes. You need to involve your audience right at the beginning. Don't start talking about laws surrounding asbestos. What is asbestos? Why is it dangerous? Tell me a story. Get me interested," I said.

One of our trainers took John into the studio and began to work with him. The story that John started to tell was fascinating: "Asbestos is found in the California state rock, serpentine. The Egyptians wrapped their mummies in asbestos binding. The Greeks used it in wicks for their temple lamps. It's actually impure magnesium silicate. It's been around for a long time. The first known victim of asbestos was a British textile worker who died of the disease in 1900. Since then, thousands have died of asbestosis and mesothelioma, victims of the microscopic, hooklike fibers that attach themselves to the lining of the lungs and abdomen."

"Have you known anyone who died of asbestos?" the trainer asked John.

"Are you kidding? My grandfather did. And my father fears he may have it. I may have it myself. The latency period is twenty years. I started in the industry when I was nineteen, before we knew about protective tanks and clothing. Now my men look like astronauts when they're working to remove it. Fifteen years ago, the guys on the job laughed at me for wearing a surgeon's mask!"

This was more like it—grim, but fascinating. Once he got started, John was hard to turn off. We let the camera run. He had put down his papers and was speaking spontaneously:

"Steve McQueen died of mesothelioma, which is cancerous.

Asbestosis isn't. People say he used to race his dirt bike near the Coalinga open pit mine. I saw a man I used to work with the other day in the supermarket. I didn't have the heart to approach him. He had an oxygen tank strapped to his wheelchair."

"Enough, enough! Now tell me something positive."

"Well, in the next couple of years the Environmental Protection Agency will have banned all products containing more than .1 percent asbestos, including asbestos cement pipe and brake lining on all cars. Asbestos can and has been replaced with other, non-lethal products—not as inexpensive or strong perhaps, but safe."

"What about asbestos in the home?"

"If your home was built before 1978, it probably contains asbestos. But unless it has been disturbed, friable we call it, it can cause no harm."

"Tell me some of the places where I might find it."

"In 'popcorn' or 'cottage cheese' ceilings, around boilers, furnaces, and heating ducts, in nine-by-nine-inch linoleum floor tiles, hot water storage tanks, shingles on your roof."

"How does it become friable?"

"Through age, neglect, sloppy storage. Workmen loosen it and leave it floating (it's invisible and lighter than air). Rats play with it in the basement. Moisture and heat catalyze it—there are so many ways."

"All right, John. Thank you very much. We've got our speech."

"What do you mean?" John looked at us as if we were nuts. He shook his papers. "What about this?"

"The sooner you let go of those papers the better. Now, do you think you can get a slide of Boris Karloff in *The Mummy*? And another of Steve McQueen in *The Great Escape*? Your audience will relate to them. It will give your speech some humor and some punch."

The next time John came to see us he had a big smile on his face: "Wait'll you see my slides. I even brought a Pet Rock. I did my thing for the guys in the office, and they loved it. They gave me lots of stories too."

John's speech was called "Red-Flagging Asbestos." It was half as long as his old one and twice as interesting. Now he stood with his hands free, talking about his life as an asbestos worker.

"The new laws are mainly to protect us, and with what we know now, we can protect you."

The good news was up front, where it belonged. Boris Karloff, Steve McQueen, and the California state rock did the rest. John was ready to talk to anyone anytime about what he knew best. This time it came from the heart.

Tough Questions

After you've learned to speak in a public setting, you need to get ready to answer audience questions. Part of speaking powerfully is being able to answer tough spontaneous questions. It was painful to watch Ann fold when we asked her, "What do you charge?" But she quickly learned there is no question you can't turn to your advantage when you know what you want to say. There are no bad questions, just bad answers.

George Thompson, who teaches police officers to communicate effectively, says, "The most dangerous weapon we all own is a cocked tongue." In our studio, we see the truth of that statement daily. We are paid to find and ask the tough questions.

You'd be surprised at the number of people thrown by a simple question like "How old are you?" or "How much money do you make?" Ask someone to explain her qualifications for a particular position: "What makes you think you're qualified to run for office, head this department, spearhead this project?" And you usually hear some sputtering. It gets really dicey when you ask, "Why do people think you're not doing a good job?" We might close with a suggested smear, like "It's hard to stay ethical with today's pressures, isn't it?" These are all tough questions, but when you've considered them and know how to respond to each one, it's not hard to diffuse their impact.

Answer "How old are you?" truthfully, with no apology. If that's too difficult, deflect the question with something like "Old enough to know better than to answer a question like that" or "It's interesting that you would ask *me* a personal question now because I was just wondering how much money *you* make?"

If you're comfortable telling how much money you make, fine. If not, deflect the question with a comment like "Not enough."

For the "What makes you think you're qualified?" question, get comfortable giving a concise answer about your background. It is also important for each of us to practice answering the question "What do you do for a living?" The answer should be no more than thirty to forty seconds in length.

To respond to a question like "Why do people think you're not doing a good job?" push for clarification. Who said that? What exactly did he say? When? Address any issues, and diffuse the question by disagreeing with the premise: "Let me tell you the kind of job I've been doing. . . ."

If you are smeared by someone, refute the smear immediately. If someone says, "It's hard to stay ethical with today's pressures," you can answer, "Not for me." Humor can also help you deflect a difficult question. I have a friend, Richard, who, when put on the spot, has been known to answer, "That's a good question, what's your next question?"

Preparation produces confidence. If you want to be able to answer tough questions, here are the guidelines. They work whether you're in a business meeting, at a party, or on a radio talk show.

GUIDELINES FOR ANSWERING DIFFICULT QUESTIONS

• Anticipate any sensitive issues, and plan what you want to say.
• Concentrate on the good news you want to transmit.
• If you need time, say, "I really can't answer that question without giving you some background information."
• If you've made a mistake, admit it and then explain your next step: "We may have made a mistake, but we must not let that cloud the real issue, which is . . ."
• Refute any incorrect statements.
• Keep your answers short. Short, direct sentences have a positive impact.
• Use humor when appropriate.

LISTENING

Most of us are better at talking than we are at listening; we need to be reminded that we have two ears and one mouth.

Good listening is an active, engaging process. Listening means paying attention not only to the speaker's words but to her tone of voice and body language as well. You listen to what's being said and to what's not being said. You listen for feelings as well as content.

You probably already know what you're going to say, but you don't know what the other person is going to say. You listen to learn about another point of view. Here's what I suggest.

LISTENING TIPS

• Give your full attention.

You know when someone is giving you his full attention. If he is distracted and looking right past you, he may be hearing you but not listening.

• Listen to what people say and how they say it.

Listen to a person's tone of voice and watch her body language while you listen to her words.

• Follow up with questions:

"I heard you say this. Am I correct?" is a great question. This allows you to check and see if you're listening accurately.

• Use open-ended questions.

If you want to get involved in the conversation, ask open-ended questions to stimulate and direct it: "What do you think of . . . ?" "Why do you feel that . . . ?" "How would you . . . ?"

If you want to end a conversation, you can start asking close-ended questions that require a "yes" or "no" answer: "Do you want . . . ?" "Do you think . . . ?" "Are you finished?"

• Stay open to the communication.

Good listeners stay neutral. When people are revealing their feelings, if you act shocked and show your disapproval, you will stop the conversation cold.

It's a sign of respect when you give your time and attention to someone and truly listen. I remember one time when I drove across town for a sales meeting. I walked into the supervisor's office, introduced myself, and asked politely, "How are you?" She looked at me carefully and answered, "Okay, I guess." She looked overwhelmed, so I replied sympathetically, "It's one of those days." Just this much concern allowed her to share with me her recent problems with a coworker. We spoke for a few minutes, I made some suggestions, and her preoccupied look vanished. I realized she was filled up when I walked in and needed to empty herself of her concerns so she could listen to what I had to say.

Each of us can develop sensitivity to read the person to whom we are speaking. If she appears distracted, give her encouragement to express what's on her mind. Only when people are present can they truly talk and listen.

CHAPTER SIX

TRUE POWER COMES FROM WITHIN

If of thy worldly goods thou are bereft
and of thy store two loaves are left,
sell one and with the dole
buy daffodils to feed thy soul.
—ANONYMOUS

P ower within is the very basis of Star Quality. It, more than anything else, brings Star Quality into your daily life. Outer Star
Quality gives you form, while inner Star Quality gives you sub-
stance. Only a deep inner connection will sustain you through difficult times; it takes power within to get you through life's lessons
with grace and balance.

Over the years, I have conducted hundreds of crisis-
management trainings for people who were confronting their challenges in the glare of the media. Without exception, the people
who were successful in handling their crises were people who had
learned to *trust themselves* and, to a greater extent, to *trust life*.
This allowed them to operate from *faith* instead of fear. I've
helped political candidates stand up to intense media scrutiny,
CEOs handle the media while shepherding their corporations out
of financial peril, and rock stars face bogus drug charges head-on.
All of them were hammered, tested, and given an opportunity to
show their mettle. They could have cracked under the pressure, as
others have, but they didn't. Each of them had already made a

deep inner connection to something greater than himself. They had faith, and they had trust born from power within. Their faith nourished them through their trials. This is what kept the attacks, the accusations, and the questioning by hoards of press in perspective.

SUSTAINING STAR QUALITY

The emphasis of our culture is directed far more to the outer self than the inner self. Television, advertising, American culture in general would lead us to believe that a beautiful outside is what's important. And it's partially true! A strong outer expression of Star Quality will get you into the room, but it will not *keep* you there.

Developing Star Quality and *sustaining* Star Quality are two completely different issues. Star Quality is *developed* on the outside and on the inside, but it's *sustained* on the inside. That's why when I work with "stars"—people with enormous talent who have clearly taken their outer expression to the limit—I look for the inner expression of their Star Quality. When they show me they have a spiritual line through to something greater than themselves, I know they are home free. Their inner essence will sustain them through all the adulation and all the outer manifestations of their Star Quality. When this inner essence is not present, I frequently see the drugs or the alcohol they use to comfort themselves to try to fill their void.

The secret is:

Power within comes from knowing that inside you there is something of value.

When you understand this, you spend time with the slower, richer, heart-centered inside of your life. Your value is established quite easily when you feel yourself part of life's *oneness*. You realize we are all part of the same race. We just come in different shapes and shades of color. The nineteenth-century Suquamish chief Seattle said this best: "Man did not weave the web of life, he is merely a strand in it. Whatever he does to the web, he does to himself."

Your value is based on the value you give yourself and on the value you give to others. The way you treat other people greatly affects how you feel about yourself. The Golden Rule is profound because it tells the truth of how life works. When "you do unto others as you would have others do unto you," you realize that:

To help someone else is to help yourself.

You begin to experience your connection to each person on this planet. They *are* your brothers and sisters. You are not isolated or alone. Each of us is a strand in the web of life. We all share the same source. We are all connected to the whole. Your value and my value are the same.

You no longer do anything that would consciously hurt another person. You honor and respect others as you do yourself. You no longer make your decisions by asking "What's the best for me?" Something shifts, and you find yourself making your decisions *for the highest good of all concerned*. You are connected not just to your needs but to the needs of others. You see the big picture and trust that there is more to life than your survival because you feel connected to something outside yourself. This is exactly how we learn to trust.

TRUST

The path to self-trust and trust in life, a higher power, God, comes as you begin to let go of the fear and anger and start to ask, "What is the lesson? Why did this happen to me? What is there here for me to learn?"

You stop fighting the magnificent teaching that is your life and start learning what you're here to learn. Growing, experiencing, learning to live your life in a happier, more fulfilled way becomes your passion. This truth jumps out at you.

Life is guiding you.

You can begin to trust in a much deeper way because you know that you are connected to something greater than yourself.

I like the way author Marianne Williamson puts it when she says, "You can let the same force that makes flowers grow and planets move run your life, or you can do it yourself."

It was through learning to trust my *natural* knowing that I noticed I had become more sensitive in my work.

Blind Faith

I use the On Camera studio to provide a series of Presence Workshops designed to help people gain confidence. The Presence Workshop starts at 9:00 A.M. on Saturdays and lasts until 5:00 P.M. One particular group was composed of eight women and four men. All looked like normal workshop participants except for a tall, stooped, bearded man who came tapping in with a cane. The workshop's eleven other participants faded into the background. A voice inside my head screamed, "My God, this is a *video* workshop and there's a blind man in here." I asked everyone to introduce themselves on camera for the first videotaped exercise. That's when I found out the man with the cane was from Santa Cruz. His name was Tom. I guessed he was about thirty. "I read about this in my Braille paper. Something told me to come here. So I got on a bus and came," he stated. Tom did not smile; there was a definite edge to him. "Perfect," I thought. "An *angry* blind guy!"

After everyone spoke, we played back the recorded statements to get a sense of how each individual felt about seeing himself or herself on the screen. Almost everyone responded with heavy self-criticism.

People who were guarded and uptight recognized it. People who were domineering knew it. Insecurity was obvious. When it was Tom's turn, I started a silent prayer, hoping there was a way to help this man.

We played the videotape, and I blocked off the picture on the television monitor. We used only our ears to hear his voice, relying on vibratory messages that usually only a blind person can "see." Sighted people, I realized, have a surplus of visual cues that distract them from voice tones.

Tom's "wall" was apparent.

"I sound kind of mean," he observed.

"Mean, Tom?"

"Yeah, mean."

"You've got an edge to your voice. You sound angry to me."

There was a moment's silence. "I'm angry because I'm blind, because I can't see."

"I can understand that. How long have you been blind?"

"A couple of months."

"How did it happen?"

"A car accident; it was instantaneous."

"You have every right to be angry! This is a lot to deal with. Have you been getting any help in Santa Cruz?"

"I have a therapist, and I'm in a counseling group," he replied.

Then I said something that just sort of rolled out of my mouth. "Tom, you are blind, but don't accept for a moment that you can't see."

"Is this a joke?" he shot back. "I'm one hundred percent nonsighted."

The anger was right there. We were on to it. But his anger was not going to solve his problem, so I switched to a more sympathetic tone: "It's so hard to let go of the anger and sadness. It feels so stuck and so bad. You're aching. I can feel your pain."

I said to the group, "Let's do an exercise now. Pair off in twos, pull your chairs to a quiet part of the room, and answer these questions for each other."

They pulled away and started to work on what each person perceived as his most "stuck" place. Could they find a way through it? What would life look like if they let go of their blocks? It was midafternoon. People were letting go. They were working on themselves. The room was alive with presence.

I went to work on Tom. Now I felt confident that I understood his issues. "Okay, Tom, you can't see because to you seeing can only be done through the eyes, right?"

"Right," he said.

"It's not the same for me, Tom. In fact, my eyes are one of my least effective means of seeing. People can mask their faces. The voice, however, carries emotion, tone, and meaning. It's much harder to mask the voice. Lie detectors read the voice, not the face.

"Often, when people talk to me, I close my eyes to 'get' them; what I'm really doing is 'sensing' them. I don't believe for a minute that people are what they say or how they look. We're deeper than that. That's where you are now, Tom. Your blindness has cut through all the superficiality of life to the heart of the matter."

A glimmer of recognition showed on his face. "Things do seem simpler now," he said.

"Do something for me. When you hear the next person, Susan, try to 'see' her."

I turned the video back on. "She's in her twenties, attractive, not too tall. She's acting younger, more insecure than she needs to," Tom said.

People's mouths dropped open. Two women began to cry. Applause broke out. He had her down pat; he knew Susan.

Next, I asked him to "see" Dan. He read him to a tee: middle-aged, a bit overweight, and tough on himself. Tom said Dan needed to relax more, to lighten up.

Someone asked him *how* he did it.

"I don't know. They're there. I guess I just sort of see them." Most people understand that intuition can't be explained through the rational mind but that it is a sixth sense available to all of us.

My hunch was right. Tom's intuition was highly developed. He enjoyed the exercise. The real work, however, was getting him to move through his anger. He was standing tall now. He seemed to accept blindness as a condition of his life. We finished our work with the other participants. As we were closing, I asked Tom if there was anything good about being blind. He responded:

"I like pretending to get my cane caught in women's skirts and lifting them up. That's fun. I'm pretty intuitive about what's underneath."

A Trust Test

My own feeling of increasing trust was giving me a lot more inner strength. I was trusting myself and what I knew on the inside. This trust was tested one dark winter night.

I had rented a house in Laguna Beach right on the water. Many weekends I would drive to Laguna and spend two or three days alone at my home. I would take long walks on the beach, meditate, read, and generally let go. One very dark, starless winter night, I had been reading upstairs, enjoying a fire. About eleven o'clock I was sleepy and walked downstairs to my bedroom. I had two windows with shades that opened onto a very small back patio. As I started to pull down the first shade, I looked through the window and saw a man outside, his face pressed to the window only inches from mine. Fear shot from my eyes to his. Clearly we were both startled. He ran, and I stood there. I heard him run down the stairs to the beach and out my open gate. I sat down on my bed. Nothing in me told me this man meant me any harm. I sensed he was a homeless Peeping Tom. So I went out the back door, down the stairs, closed my gate, and went to bed. The gate was not what made me feel secure. There was only a two-foot wall around the sides of the house. He could have entered on either side. I felt secure and protected in my heart. I knew this man was harmless to me. I went to sleep amazed at how strong I felt inside and how happy I was that I was learning to listen and trust the higher spiritual voice inside me. I knew how to listen to my gut. I trusted myself. Because of all the work I had been doing on myself—the meditation, the workshops, the therapy—I was getting stronger on the inside. I was developing trust.

Just when I thought I was so good at sensing people and being able to tell intuitively the good and bad of things, I was blindsided by a lesson in trusting others.

Trusting Other People

I had always considered myself a careful person who evaluated people before I put my trust in them. Like everyone else, I had been hurt in the past when I trusted someone too easily. Many times I quoted an old Arab maxim: "Trust everyone, and tie your camel." I was ripe for a spiritual test. About this time, I hired a new secretary. She presented herself as a talented and considerate person. She taught Sunday school, raised chickens, and had a vegetable garden. She was also a wiz on the computer and very attentive to detail. I was impressed and began to trust her more and more with the business side of On Camera. Ten months later, I needed to track down a canceled check for the Department of Motor Vehicles and Claire couldn't produce it. I started looking through my checkbook and saw some other irregularities. I confronted Claire, and the next morning she responded with a call from her lawyer, who admitted that she was an embezzler. She had stolen $60,000 from my personal and business accounts.

This was a devastating lesson for me. Up until this time, I thought that because I was a good person, life would protect me from its evils. I couldn't understand how this could have happened. I was overwhelmed with feelings of betrayal and loss. My feelings would move back and forth from helplessness to rage and anger.

After I got over the shock I started looking back to see how I could have let this occur. Where did I go wrong? What was this painful lesson? Why did it happen?

I knew myself to be a person who always looked on the good side of things. I cared about people enormously and was easily taken in by Claire's lies. Her stories of having Hodgkin's disease and various emotional problems had prompted me to help her. I was easy prey for someone's evil manipulation. Victims, I realized, are people who have not learned to deal with the dark, or shadow, side of their own life. I was seeing life the way I wanted it to be and ignoring the reality. As a result of this lesson, I realized I had not faced *my* shadow of self-deprivation. I liked to save money, hoard it even. I continually saved and underspent. Because I denied myself the pleasure of money, it was sitting there available for someone else to enjoy. It was hard to admit that I had created this problem out of my own insecurity and fear.

Claire had withheld lots of information while working for me. She was very controlling, and I'd found it increasingly uncomfortable to be around her. Yet I hadn't wanted to face rehiring and retraining someone else. My intuitive beeper had been going off for some time, but I couldn't hear it. I kept making adjustments—even paying for her to get help—convincing myself I could work with her. Now I realize that I don't want to work with people with whom I don't feel good. Of course, one should help others—but it never works to help someone else at your own emotional expense.

Claire helped me wake up to the knowledge that I had never faced evil. I was so busy cultivating the light, bright side of life that I had not reckoned with the dark side.

Good and Evil

When my son was six, he attended Sunday school, where his teacher always talked about God. One Sunday Zack said to her, "I've heard enough about God. Let's talk about something I'm interested in. Let's talk about the devil."

A year later, I was called to his school by the principal, who was concerned because Zack had been cheating on a school paper and then lied about having done it. We were sitting in the principal's office when I asked Zack, "Why are you behaving like this?"

"Look, Mom," he replied, "I've been good for a long time. It's time I tried being bad."

I was watching my son grapple with good and evil. He seemed to be trying to resolve both parts inside himself. He did not want to cut himself off from his shadow, or dark, side.

Now I understood why my son was so interested in his shadow side. Only by facing it in himself and in the world could he ever hope to be whole. We need to get in touch with our dark side, explore it, and acknowledge our shadow parts. Good and evil, light and dark, joy and sorrow all coexist as opposite values. There is always duality. I stopped seeing things as either black or white and started noticing that the world is all shades of gray. We experience life through contrast. Therefore, one is necessary for the experience of the other.

Months later, a friend and I were having breakfast and he showed me an article in *The Times* of London that referred to him as the Prince of Darkness. I said, "Great. You're facing another part of you. I have found that until each of us deals with our own darkness we can never spread the light."

Years later, as I view this lesson, it is clear to me that we need opposition to grow. Before all this happened, I didn't pay a lot of attention to money matters. I left that to the embezzlers. Now, of course, I am grounded in the reality that people lie, cheat, steal, even kill each other over money. I trust my new office manager, bookkeeper, and accountant, but I also check my records regularly. I am far more trusting of people now than I was before the Claire incident. The reason is, I no longer ignore my feelings and try to cut myself off from the darkness in someone else and the darkness inside me. It's much easier to trust others when you learn to trust yourself. As your trust increases, you aren't emotionally attached to all your problems. You begin to gain distance from them. You detach.

DETACHMENT

Evelyn is a musician and singer who uses On Camera to go over her show routines before she performs her concerts onstage. She came running into our studio one day shouting, "Life is carrying me, life is carrying me. Everything is moving, and I feel safe. It's exquisite. What a feeling." She had written a song that came straight from her heart, she told me, but more than this, everything in her life was flowing.

"What did you do?" I asked her.

"Nothing," she replied. "I just trust God totally in everything. I gave up the struggle, that's all."

I had watched Evelyn handle the business of life. She'd always been able to deal with little problems, but it was wonderful now to see her joy. "How would you describe how you feel?" I asked her.

"I have let go of fear. I am in a state of grace. I'm flying."

"Evelyn, it sounds like you have a lot of detachment and trust, but you're also not facing any real adversity," I said.

"That's not true. My mother is sick. I have been flying home every weekend to care for her. It's sometimes hard on my husband, but I tell him, 'This is the best I can do right now.'"

"Does he understand?" I asked.

"Yes. He knows I feel strongly that all events, everything that happens to us in life, is brought to us for our growth. I need this time with my mother. Bill knows I have enough love inside of me for my mother and for him. Maybe not enough time [she laughed], but enough love."

"You are handling this very well," I commented.

"That's because I feel the presence of God inside of me. I have nothing to fear. Life is evolving just as it should. I am being carried just as the planets are carried in space."

I smiled at Evelyn. She started humming one of her heart songs.

Evelyn had *mastered* detachment and trust. Because she felt this deep trust, she was experiencing the comfort, the high, that comes from gaining a *connection* to something greater than yourself, a power within.

Evelyn had made a powerful connection to the God force. Other people have described this feeling as a oneness experience.

Oneness

It's only in the past few years that friends and clients have begun sharing their "oneness experiences" with me. These occur when a person experiences a feeling of *deep connection* to something greater than himself. These experiences have included near death, out-of-body travel to heavenly realms, angels appearing and communicating through thought forms, and meditations that brought revelations of peace and grace. A friend, Catherine, had what I would call a typical oneness experience.

Catherine had felt lost and was in tremendous pain when she sat under a tree in her backyard weeping. "I was weeping, praying, pleading, when all of a sudden an explosion occurred inside my head. In one instant, I had answers to all my questions. The answers were layered on top of each other. It was as if I could feel and think at the same time. The words had thickness and comfort to them. They came as a divine spark that shot through my body and brought me amazing peace. I had been spoken to, touched by a force so powerful and knowing that I knew that I was watched over and loved. I also knew I had something very special inside of me."

The beauty of such experiences is that they profoundly connect you up to a power or force greater than yourself. We may not all have a oneness experience, yet each of us can learn to live in the present moment—which is the only place where Star Quality exists.

STAYING PRESENT

The essence of Star Quality is expressed in the present moment. This is the only place where you can experience power within. Relax into the present. Don't spend time wandering back into the past or escaping into dreams of the future. Enjoy the *here and now*. The past is gone; the future has yet to occur; only the present moment exists. Here you are free to act, to move forward in your life, to create the life you want to live. Here you are empowered.

Because of fear, our minds may try to keep us locked in the past, remembering some old memory, or fixated on the future, living in a state of constant anticipation. Fear is all that keeps us from being in the present moment where happiness exists.

When you're living in the present, you're not fantasizing about what your life would be like if you got a raise or found a mate. You don't care much about what your life *used* to be like. You're right here in this moment, experiencing, feeling, acting, being alive. This moment holds your power. This is where things happen.

Learning to stay present is a skill that requires practice. Zen Buddhists define learning to be awake in the present moment as "mindfulness." Think about walking. Many times we use it merely as a means of getting somewhere. What if you were to become involved in the very act of walking? You would start to be aware of every step, the feel of your feet on the ground, the swing of your arms, the feeling of the air on your skin. Mindfulness can be learned and practiced as a way to bring you right into the present moment.

Living in the present doesn't mean you never think about the past or the future. It's natural to have past thoughts, future thoughts, all *kinds* of thoughts pass through your mind. The challenge is not to dwell on them. You want to stay open to the present, which requires that you not get stuck too long in any one thought. To live in the present, you must delight in the simple moments of the day—your morning coffee, the ride to work, talking with a friend.

CENTERING

It's your inner power that allows you to express your outer Star Quality. To stay trusting, detached, and in the present moment, you need to use spiritual practices to nourish your spirit. Shopping, watching television, and eating will not get you in touch with your center. You need to make daily connections to that which is greater than you are. This is called *centering*.

Spiritual practices are the paths or ways you use to connect yourself up to the whole so you no longer feel separate but part of the greater oneness of life. You are part of the rhythm of the world. Your life matters. How you live it is important. These spir-

MINDFULNESS EXERCISE

Begin your mindfulness as you start the day. Give your wholehearted attention to whatever you are doing in each moment. For instance, when you are showering, your attention is only on washing your body. Slowing down this activity helps you observe the process more precisely. You may silently repeat "washing, washing" in order to keep yourself focused on washing your body. Whatever you are doing must be the sole focus of your attention. Many people miss this daily moment because they're thinking about the upcoming day. Truly being in this moment carries with it a cleansing, rejuvenating sensation.

When you're drinking tea, practice feeling the cup. Pour the tea. Taste the tea. Focus on drinking the tea. If your mind wanders, repeat "drinking, drinking" to pull yourself back to the present.

Eating a piece of fruit is an excellent way to practice mindfulness. For example, choose a tangerine. Look at the tangerine, then smell it, feel it, peel it. Bring it up slowly to your mouth, and be aware of the saliva that is beginning to secrete inside your mouth. Put a piece of tangerine into your mouth and begin to taste it. Slowly enjoy the practice of eating a tangerine.

To keep centered in the present moment, practice mindfulness several times a day.

itual practices bring you back to your center when you are being challenged—and they keep you centered when you are delightfully experiencing the rhythmic flow.

Spiritual Practices

You need to be able to find a way to tap into something greater than yourself so you can surrender to your experiences and learn from them. If you are looking for an opening so you can hear that still, small voice within, prayer and meditation are a good place to start.

The Power of Prayer

Prayer puts you in partnership with God, whatever you conceive God to be, whether Mother God, or Father God, or your Higher Power. You pray, you ask, you thank; you pray for grace and for the ability to forgive.

Prayer, like meditation, is there so we can touch a power greater than ourselves. "Thy will be done" is the most powerful prayer I know. It gets ego out of the way and puts me in a place of surrender to a higher power, to God. It allows me to feel humbly in touch with my own divinity.

I have learned to pray for the strength to let go of my will and to surrender to "Thy will be done." I pray to understand my lessons so I can more easily find the way down my path and continue growing. I pray when I am hurt or in pain and need help finding my way back to my center. I pray with thankfulness and gratitude for all my blessings.

One of my clients, a minister, said, "Too many people pray very actively to God, letting Him know exactly what they want. But I find they're so busy praying, they forget to listen for the answer. It's through our attentive silence that we receive messages from God . . . that we hear what God wants." He understood that it's through silence and meditation that we receive both truth and strength.

Meditation

When I first started On Camera, I asked each client, "What do you do to relax yourself and counteract stress?" Many people answered, "I go for a walk" or "I take a hot bath." Very few ever mentioned meditation. That has all changed. Today I frequently hear, "I go into silence. I meditate." One client explained it perfectly: "All the activities of my day pull me away from the peace and joy that is inside me. I get back to it through meditation. Here I experience my essence."

Prayer and meditation are the ultimate spiritual practices. They not only connect you up to something greater than yourself, they help bring peace and harmony into your life. This is why they are the true building blocks of inner Star Quality.

I find waking up in the morning to be a good time to get connected to the peace and joy inside me. The chatter inside our minds can be filled with thoughts of fear and pain. Meditation gives you the distance to detach from your problems. As you meditate regularly, you begin to connect to the true nature of your spirit, which is the joy inside you. It's best to meditate at least twenty minutes two times a day, once upon rising and either before dinner or later that night. There are many different ways to meditate. Experiment and see what works best for you. Here are the simple steps I use.

STEPS FOR BEGINNING MEDITATION

1. Sit in a relaxed body posture so you feel comfortable with your back, neck, and head in a straight vertical line. Uncross your arms and legs. Place your hands on your knees. Keep your face relaxed as you put an ever-so-slight smile on it.

(continued)

---

2. Close your eyes. Bring your attention to your breathing. Observe your breath as it flows in and out. Focus on your heart area. Breathe in and out, focusing on your heart. Breathe deeply.

3. To do a Ham-Sa meditation, breathe in to the interior sound "hum" and breathe out to the sound "saw." Gently repeat "hum-saw" in your mind to the rhythm of your breathing. "Hum" for the incoming breath. "Saw" for the outgoing breath. Notice the space between breaths.

4. Let yourself feel the peace. If thoughts interrupt you, let them pass and gently move back to Ham-Sa. The peace you feel will replace your desire to think.

5. Continue this practice for approximately twenty minutes. Then gently let yourself come back to your day. Take several minutes to open your eyes, stretch your body, and ease back into your life.

Use meditation to let go of the day's stresses and connect to the joy and the peace inside you. There are two other practices that will help keep you centered. The first involves communing with nature.

Mother Nature
Mother Nature has amazing restorative powers. The green-blue healing power of plants and lakes, the inspirational pinks and oranges of sunrises and sunsets, the nourishing warmth of the sun, the cleansing of a cool rain, the expansiveness of the big sky, and the rhythm of the sea are all there to assist us in healing, balancing, and centering ourselves.

You can use the natural rhythms of nature to calm yourself after a stressful day. When you walk over soft ground into a forest, you realize that everything in the forest always seems to be all right with itself. You don't get the feeling that an oak tree wishes it were a pine or a fern wishes it were a mushroom. In nature things are perfect just as they are. And that's exactly how I feel when I'm in touch with nature. If the birds are singing or squawking, it's fine with me. And even when animals kill other animals, I remind myself there is a food chain and this is the natural order of things.

I have spent some of the most satisfying days of my life communing with Mother Nature—listening, smelling, touching, watching, and generally feeling one with the rhythms of this amazing planet.

When you need recharging, go outside. Walk among the trees. Lie on the grass and feel the sun shine on you. Take a swim in a lake or the sea. Gaze appreciatively at the mountains. Let the earth's elements powerfully affect you. Enjoy the beauty of this planet. It is a living organism that supports your life. Give it your reverence.

The second practice allows you to slow down and retreat from the hustle of life.

Keeping the Sabbath
We are all so busy. Going, doing, talking, getting, spending . . . it just goes on and on. One day a week we need to stop and disconnect from our day-to-day life. We are so into action that we need one day a week to refrain from acting upon the world. This is the day to stand back, admire, and celebrate the grandeur of life.

One day a week, which you may want to take on Saturday or Sunday, take a retreat from your daily life. Don't work, fix anything, shop, or even drive much. Stay home, read, walk, hike in nature, laugh with friends, or play with your children. The rule is: Don't do any work. Attend to the quieter things of the spirit.

THREE INNER STAR QUALITIES

There are three obvious qualities that bespeak a power within. First, there's an **inner radiance** that ignites the imagination. I have seen this in priests and yogis, in spiritual people, but lately I have been noticing it in corporate honchos and people in the arts. I can't exactly put my finger on why this is, but I've noticed there is a certain trust in the vagaries of life that people have developed. They don't question everything but rather seem to have a peaceful acceptance of the way things are. One client, a megasuccessful actress, put it this way: "I trust that I'm always in the right place at the right time." What she means, from a practical standpoint, is that she's able to face the challenges that life gives her eagerly, which, in turn, brings a lightheartedness and a light within her that is a delight to behold.

The second quality one develops is true **inner strength**. I got a phone call from a sad-sounding sixteen-year-old girl named Sarah. Her pain and confusion were palpable. Both her parents were public figures whose lives had been broadcast all over the tabloids. There was a huge family scandal involving millions of dollars. The press was hungry for information. Reporters had approached her, and Sarah wanted to know if she should tell her story. "I am so very hurt by my father. What should I say?" she asked.

"How do you feel?" I replied.

"I feel that there was some wrongdoing on the part of my dad. The truth may never come out, but something is not right," she continued. "I'm not sure I want to trash him publicly. He's human. We all get off the track from time to time." As painful as her parents' feud was for Sarah, she was already showing compassion for both of them.

I asked her, "Do you think if you discussed it publicly that this would further invade your family's privacy?"

She mumbled, "Yes. And I believe we actually might be able to heal our problems. So much is out in the open now. This could serve as a catalyst to bring us closer together." She was a teenager, yet so sensitive that she considered her parents' problems her own. Sarah decided, "This is a family matter, and it will have to be healed by the power of love."

I was impressed that she had wisdom beyond her years. Her compassion and love came from deep within. It was refreshing to experience her depth. She had been raised in a materialistic outer-directed home, yet she had demonstrated true inner strength.

Without exception, people who have power within have developed a third quality, *a generosity of spirit*. They feel passionately about their work in the world and have an uncommon faith in themselves and their ability to make a contribution to the world's welfare. Star Quality compels one to shine his or her light into the world. Whether Jimmy and Rosalyn Carter are building Habitat Homes for low-income families or Paul Newman is donating all the profits from Newman's Own to charity or Sting is giving his annual concert to save the rain forest—true stars give! They give Live Aid and they give Comic Relief.

I was driving down Twenty-sixth Street in Santa Monica when I noticed one of our former star clients in front of me. I beeped, and he waved me over. We hadn't seen each other in years, and almost immediately he started regaling me with this story:

"Do you know about the children's hospital I'm helping to build?" he asked.

I didn't, so he told me.

He was hosting benefits and fund-raisers, even tithing 10 percent of his movie grosses in his effort to raise the millions of dollars it would take to build this hospital, whose special purpose was to heal disadvantaged children from all parts of the world.

I said, "You're so busy. I know from the newspapers that you just finished shooting a movie. Now you're spending all your time on this huge benefit. How do you do it?"

He answered me straight: "Life is good to me. I'm getting so much out of life, I want to put it back in." This is characteristic of power within. You want to help others because your own life works. There is always a generosity of spirit.

CHAPTER SEVEN

You Deserve

Star

Treatment

Everybody is a star, doesn't matter who you are.
—SLY STONE

Star Treatment starts with *you*. When you appreciate and take good care of yourself, you're going to expect and *get* the same treatment from others.

SELF-LOVE: THE KEY TO STAR QUALITY

By now, it will come as no surprise to you when I say the key to Star Quality is self-love. Star Quality occurs when an inner expression of self-love matches an outer expression of power and presence.

Making a decision to star in your own life is very empowering. You are committed to loving yourself. You have no trouble walking into any situation and feeling "I am of value." When Lena Horne says, "I can honestly say I believe in me," she epitomizes personal power. She even closes her act with "I Believe in You," from *The Wiz*.

As you develop your Star Quality, your power and magnetism

naturally expand. It's a strong sense of your own unique presence that brings you personal magnetism. Star Quality means you become aware of your originality and uniqueness. As you begin to acknowledge your value, you realize that natural self-love has nothing to do with self-centeredness, conceit, or egotism. In fact, it's precisely *because* you value and respect yourself that you are able to know the worth and importance of other human beings.

By acknowledging who and what you are, you are able to accept a realistic picture of yourself. True stars don't focus on what they *don't* have. Instead, they understand that they are stars precisely because of what they *do* have.

Each of us needs to do the work to heal ourselves. We owe it to ourselves to let go of our critical self-judgments and limiting beliefs. Free yourself so you can see yourself objectively, and appreciate yourself for who you are. It's a nourishing, joyful place to be. One of my clients described it as perfection.

PERFECTION AND SELF-WORTH

During one of our sessions, Susan said, "I know that I am perfect." I smiled and replied, "The dictionary defines perfect as 'something that has all the properties that naturally belong to it.' It sounds like you have all the properties that belong to you." "That's not what I mean," she replied. "What I mean is I see the perfection of my imperfections. I am no longer discontent with my imperfections. I just see them as me, what is uniquely me." I was thrilled to hear her say this. She was defining self-acceptance.

Listening to her reminded me of the story of the most perfect hunchback. A minister was standing in front of his congregation, preaching his Sunday sermon. The topic was man's perfection. The preacher shouted, "You are all perfect. God loves you just as you are. You are perfect, perfect." There was a rustle as a man with a hunchback stood up and shouted from the back of the room, "What about me, pastor?" The preacher paused, then replied, "Brother, you are the most perfect hunchback I have ever seen!"

Both Susan and the preacher understood that the way to experience Star Quality is to understand this:

Appreciate your own unique presence so that you are inspired by your experience of yourself.

As you experience your self-worth, you value yourself, you celebrate your successes, and you notice all the ways you are growing into a better person.

Susan is a woman I have known for almost ten years. During this time, I have watched her learn how to love and appreciate herself. Today, she is expert at giving and receiving star treatment.

"I value myself and others," she said. "I have finally learned to express myself, to speak my feelings without putting myself or anyone else down. Treating each person with love and respect takes care of myself, and it also takes care of others."

She continued, "Each day, I make time just for myself. No husband. No kids. Just me. It doesn't matter if I use the time to read, or take a class, or meditate. I have learned how important it is not to give all my energy away to others but to reserve some time to replenish myself and give back to me."

Susan understands that there needs to be a balance between what is going on inside and outside you. This happens when you are aware of your own true value.

RULES OF SELF RESPECT

• Respect your own feelings just as you respect the feelings of others.
• Be aware of yourself and your needs just as you are aware of the needs of others.
• Be generous with yourself in the same way you are generous with others.

Knowing your own value helps carry you through life's more challenging times. I saw this work with Ariel, who used self-love to carry her through a difficult test involving jealousy. Ariel is a beautiful woman who used her recent divorce as an opportunity to get into therapy and work on herself. She came to On Camera to work on developing her presence. Here is her story as she relayed it to me:

"I met a man and fell in love. I felt very vulnerable. We went to the theater, and he told me that his ex-lover, who had left him and who he wanted to have children with, was sitting in the audience with the man who broke down his door four months ago and took her away from him.

"My stomach got tight, and I immediately thought of my beauty, which saves me from so much fear and also gives me fear. At intermission, I dove for the ladies' room to see that I was all right. Thank God. I looked terrific. I returned to the foyer and stood there with the love of my life. Then we saw his ex-lover. I was totally unprepared for this platinum-blond, to-the-waist hair, features with perfect symmetry, flawless skin, wearing an up-to-the-minute WWD ensemble that loomed in front of me. Her hand jutted out, and with a perfect smile she said, 'Hi, I'm Diana.'

"I don't know if he told her my name because I was really overcome by her beauty. My name was a real blur to me anyway. I felt so intimidated. I was spared the verbal exchange between my lover, his ex-lover, and the man who broke down the door. Some man on my right was speaking to me about New York or Washington or his mother. I was forgetting to breathe and finding it hard to focus without air. The lights flashed. We moved back to our seats, and I made an attempt to be light when I was in shock (which never works) so the things that I said were stupid. He didn't talk at all, which was smart.

"Jealousy had unfocused everything for me. I had pie-in-the-face knowledge that there are beautiful, younger women than I who have energy pulls to the man I love. It was then that I realized that I have only whoever I know I am *inside*. Amazingly, I felt intact. I realized that I am *more* than my looks. The mirror can't help me assuage my jealousy nor can any of my talents or possessions. I felt enormously vulnerable and yet open to the possibility that I may be enough. My looks may just be my looks, my heart, however weak or strong, my heart. Yes, *I am enough*. Something inside me is calm and wise and willing to let nature take its course."

Ariel had done the work on herself, and when she met a challenging situation, she was able to dig down deep and know her value. She had learned to accept herself, and jealousy could not diminish her. She had self-worth.

LIFEWORK

Work either increases your self-worth or decreases it. It adds or subtracts value from your life. Your work needs to be fulfilling. And in order for this to happen, you must build your career around something you love to do. Obviously, we all need to make a living, but working *just* to make money can be a very draining experience.

Many people are in an unfulfilling profession because they bought into the myth that your work defines your worth. They work in a family business not because they want to but because they are expected to. They become doctors or lawyers not because they felt a call to heal or seek justice but because medicine and law are high-status professions.

When you work *just* for money or status, you lose the satisfaction that comes from developing your own unique abilities and God-given talents. A good question to ask yourself is "What work could I do that would make me a success to myself?"

Each person has something unique to contribute to the world. To attain Star Quality, that contribution doesn't need to be a Nobel Prize–winning scientific breakthrough. It *does* need to be something you feel drawn to, something you *believe* in. You do need to feel that what you are doing is meaningful.

I have an artist client who is so inspired by his work that he tells me, "My work is worship." Most people don't feel quite this ecstatic about their job, though. They're more like my mechanic, Bill.

Bill really enjoys working on cars. He's been fixing them since he was a kid. When you go to see him, his garage is clean (for a garage), he has a smile on his face, and he takes good care of your car. Everything he says he can do he does on time and for a fair price.

Contrast Bill with a guy who has a dirty garage and a bad attitude. He overbids your job, fixes your car, and, one month later, it breaks down again.

Bill is making a contribution. He enjoys his work and does his best to give you great service. He found his career out of a genuine interest, not because his dad owned a garage or because he thought it was an easy way to make money. His work as a mechanic serves both himself and others.

You can be in any type of work or profession and make a contribution to yourself and others. I know CEOs of Fortune 500 companies who gain great satisfaction from their work. They enjoy steering their companies into profitability, but they also demand that their corporations be good corporate citizens. Advertising men and women who enjoy coming up with creative ideas, gardeners who love working outdoors with plants, social workers who gain satisfaction from helping others have all built their careers around something they love to do. Several years ago, there was an article in the *Los Angeles Times* about a supermarket checkout boy who knew how to enjoy his work. Customers would drive ten minutes out of their way to come to his store and stand in his line. He joked with his customers, told them stories, teased them about their food choices. He really made his job fun!

More people die from heart attacks at 9:00 A.M. Monday morning than at any other time, which proves that the wrong kind of work can be dangerous to your health. If you don't believe in what you're doing and you don't find satisfaction in your work, you're doing the wrong thing. Look at your job closely. If it is subtracting from your life rather than adding to it, maybe it's time to make a change.

As we grow through life, our desires grow too. When I was in my twenties, nothing was more interesting to me than studying and working in the field of psychology. I didn't know it then, but as I look back now, I realize my primary interest and desire was to heal myself. As I got healthier, I became interested in finding a way to work with people. I was in my mid-thirties when I had the inspiration to help people develop their personal power and founded On Camera. Now, at fifty, I'm writing about what I've discovered. In the twenty-five years I've been working, I have had three distinct career changes, all reflecting my own personal development and the growth of my interests.

Find work you can look forward to doing. When you find what you are meant to be doing in the world, you'll find you have the power to do it very well.

TAKING CARE OF YOURSELF

You can increase your feelings of self-worth simply by taking good care of yourself. It takes health and energy to project Star Quality. Let's look at Star Quality energy robbers and energy boosters.

Energy Robbers

Star Quality is not static. It increases or decreases depending on the inner and outer strength we have developed. Therefore, it's essential to become aware of what adds or subtracts from the energy you have available to you. Energy, after all, is a very important commodity. It's your usable power. Let's look at some common energy robbers.

Stress

Star Quality's number one enemy is stress. Stress will shut your Star Quality right down. A nervous, stressed-out person is going to have a very hard time letting his Star Quality shine.

Phones, faxes, expressways—we live a fast-paced existence. Information comes at us at a dazzling speed. World problems, national problems, and local problems zoom into our minds through radio and television. Sirens wail, kids cry, and angry people get right in our face. Just the speed with which our society moves is a lot to handle.

The stress of daily life puts lots of physical demands on our body. These demands, of course, go hand in hand with mental demands. In order to maintain any sort of equilibrium, it is essential to manage the way your body handles stress.

We recommend using the tense and release your muscles exercise from chapter two and the rhythmic breathing exercise and the neck relaxation exercises in this chapter. Meditation, which is discussed in chapter six, is also extraordinarily helpful for managing life's stresses. It's through relaxation that you learn to regulate your tight stomach and clenched jaw. By relaxing yourself, you can slow down these stress responses—or even turn them off.

There are two types of relaxation: *therapeutic* and *cathartic*. Therapeutic relaxation consists of such activities as meditation, rhythmic breathing, and yoga stretches. Cathartic relaxation consists of physical exercise, such as aerobics, sports, and walking. Therapeutic relaxation techniques are used to slow things down. Cathartic exercises are what you do to blow off steam.

Many of us are used to living at a high stress level, so we need to check into our body to see how we're doing. Here's an exercise similar to the muscle tense and release exercise in chapter two. I like to use it to check my body for tension.

STRESS SCAN EXERCISE

When you're sitting down with a few minutes to spare, scan your body for tension. Mentally examine your feet, legs, hips, stomach, chest, arms, hands, shoulders, neck, and head. Become aware of these areas one at a time, and see if you can detect tension building. When you locate an area of tension, take a breath, hold it, and, one at a time, tense the muscle group even more. Tense it. Hold it. Now exhale and let the muscle go limp. Feel the tenseness leaving your body.

There are many ways to counteract stress, from breathing techniques and meditation to physical exercise. I also recommend a very simple antistress "activity"—doing nothing. When you feel overwhelmed, from time to time try kicking back and doing nothing at all. Lie under the shade of a tree, turn the lights off and sit in total silence—it's good for the soul. It's important that, occasionally, you achieve nothing. This is good, old-fashioned goofing-off time. It can be done at a beach, a park, a lake; you can just stare up at the clouds in the sky. Let your mind roll. Doing nothing is actually time well spent; you're taking a break and recharging your batteries.

Diet

In order to manage stress, you need to have a diet program that works for you. It takes energy to express Star Quality. What you eat can either rob or boost your energy. You don't have to have heard of the "Twinkie defense" to understand that diet plays an important role in health and energy. You may not think you are what you eat, but the food you put in your body has a huge impact on your health. Poor eating habits affect both your mood and energy levels.

Several months ago, I reviewed a videotape of an author's talk-show appearance and observed him speaking lifelessly to the host. His energy level read as sluggish. I saw that his stomach was extended, and he looked as if he were about to burp. I told him, "I see you managed to get lunch in before the taping."

Digestion takes lots of energy; the body slows down to get the food digested. If you're looking to increase your Star Quality energy, what you eat affects how you feel, which means food directly relates to the star power you project.

DIET DIRECTIONS

There is no single diet that works for everyone. You need to figure out which foods work best for you and which foods negatively affect you.

1. Eat at least three healthy, balanced meals a day. Four to six small meals spread evenly throughout the day will help keep your blood sugar level steady. Low blood sugar can cause irritability and fatigue.

2. Sugar and caffeine can negatively impact you. Even a small amount of sugar can send some people into a mood swing. Caffeine will give you an initial lift, but it may leave you feeling grouchy a few hours later. A piece of fruit is a healthy way to boost your energy.

3. Along with eating at least three healthy, balanced meals, a complete vitamin-mineral supplement should cover any deficiencies in your diet.

4. Drink plenty of water throughout the day to keep your body hydrated and cleansed. For some people, dehydration causes headaches and sluggishness.

Energy Boosters

Nature's Seven Doctors

In order to keep yourself healthy and your energy strong, follow Nature's Seven Doctors.

These "doctors" are plenty of fresh air, fresh water, proper rest, exercise, sunlight, healthy food, and a positive mental attitude. These are the health essentials that build a strong body and a strong immune system. Let's look at some ways we can give our body Star Treatment.

Physical Exercise

How much time during the day do you spend thinking, exercising your mind? The answer is: a lot! Most of us put such a high priority on mental exercise that our energy gets trapped in our heads and our poor bodies are left to drag along throughout the day.

When I put clients on camera and they seem sluggish, speaking in a monotone and wearing a generally flat countenance, immediately I say to them, "You don't have time to exercise, do you?" They give me the standard excuses—working too hard, not enough time, traveling too much—to which I say, "Working on Star Quality is not only time-consuming, it's expensive. If you put such a high priority on your mental exercise program, so that there's no time for physical exercise, then all of your energy is focused in your mind. Your body looks uninspired and lifeless. Unless you are willing to begin a concentrated exercise program right now, I am going to save you the time and money involved in this training because neither of us will get the results we want."

Everyone spends time in front of other people, whether at a family gathering, a parent-teacher conference, or a job interview. All performance situations, no matter how simple, require you to have physical vitality in order to project your Star Quality.

Physical strength boosts your ability to express yourself. Your body thrives when demands are put on it. And your life tends to improve—mentally, not just physically—when your body improves.

Fitness begins with movement. Death is total nonmovement, so it follows that more movement brings more life. To get more movement into your day, walk whenever you can, forgo the elevator and climb the stairs, garden, dance. You can swim, take aerobic classes, play tennis—just make sure you do thirty minutes of moderate-intensity physical activity three to five days a week. This is the minimum you need for Star Quality vitality. If your body is exercised but tight, consider massage therapy to get out the kinks.

NECK RELAXATION EXERCISES

In most people, the head, neck, and shoulders are prime places for the body to store stress. The tense and release your muscles exercise in chapter two and these neck relaxation exercises help release stress.

1. To relax and let the tension out of your shoulders, stand and let your arms hang at your sides. Thrust your shoulders as far back as they go and hold for a count of five. Relax. Now thrust them forward for another count of five. Relax. Repeat three times.

2. To unwind your neck, sit in a comfortable position. Slowly turn your head to look left. Then look right. Slowly move your head so you are looking at the ceiling and then at the floor. Roll your head in a full circle, stopping and holding the stretch wherever it feels tight. Now roll your head the other way. Relax and release the tension in your neck.

Massage Therapy

When tension gets stuck in your neck, shoulders, head, or anywhere else in your body, yoga, stretch exercises, and massage therapy are all very helpful in getting rid of stress and adding free-flowing energy. Skilled body workers can release energy blocked in your muscles and leave you feeling relaxed and stress-free. There are many excellent methods available, from deep tissue massage to acupressure, or shiatsu. Try different techniques to see what works best for you.

You have just learned how to give Star Treatment to your body. Now, what about your mind?

Energy Pumping

You can boost your energy by pumping it mentally and emotionally. Here's an example of how it's done:

A singer is about to go onstage. He has been on the road for weeks, and he is exhausted. Cedar Rapids . . . Green Bay . . . Milwaukee . . . The cities have become a patchwork quilt of amphitheaters, greasy food, and sleepless nights. The hamburger he gulped down hours before is still lying heavily in his stomach. Backstage, while his supporting act warms up the sellout audience, he wearily puts on his makeup and arbitrates a bitter disagreement between the head of his film production crew and a concert arena official. He hears his cues. As he leaves his dressing room, he takes a breath, makes a fist, and uses an exercise to optimize his emotions and move him into his most resourceful state. By the time he walks onstage, he is a stick of dynamite.

Salespeople, speakers, and public performers all know they need to find a way to pump and move their energy from wherever it is to a high level. If you want to inspire or touch people, you need to communicate from the highest possible emotional tone. The word *enthusiasm* comes from the Greek root word *entheos*, meaning godlike, which explains why, when you're projecting enthusiasm, it's almost impossible to resist you.

Performers know it's not difficult to shift from one energy level to another. I remember watching this happen when I was hired to interview a well-known fitness personality for a promotional tape to introduce the new exercise video he was making. He had been working all day and late into the night for three days straight. To top it off, my interview with him wasn't set until the end of the last day's shooting. He was exhausted and short-tempered. He snapped, "Christen, how long is this going to take?" And I thought, "This is going to be a disaster. The last thing he's up for is an interview." But I doggedly ran through the line of questions with him. The director gave me my cue, the floor manager counted me in, the cameras were rolling. I asked my first question: "Why is exercise so important to you?" Presto! With an instant glowing confidence, he looked straight into the camera eye and said, "Jane Fonda's got this fabulous body. Obviously, I have to come up with something more appealing. . . ." He laughed, he charmed, and he played to the camera. Even though he was drained, he had taught himself to tap into his reserves and pump his energy up at will. He knew how to turn it on.

Robin Williams is a good example of dynamic energy . . . he is enthusiasm in action. A few years ago, I was watching him entertain two friends and myself at a party and was amazed by his ability to move instantaneously into characters, voices, and scenarios. He is a comedic dynamo. I wondered if he ever shuts it off. That question was answered for me when I discovered we were both studying yoga with Alan Finger. Yoga teaches you to let go, relax, and find the balance between rest and activity.

Many of us are good at getting ourselves stuck in a low-energy place, into our *least* resourceful energy state. We start visualizing all the bad things that can happen; we pick one, magnify the fear, and work ourselves into a real panic. Believe me, this is not a state you want to create.

But what if you knew how to generate a powerful emotional and physical condition that you could re-create whenever you wanted? You can. That condition is called an "optimum resource state," and reaching it is exactly what neurolinguistic programming teaches us to do.

Here is a simple exercise that shows you how to put yourself into an empowered state. Practice this exercise until you feel comfortable that you can shift your energy and "turn it on."

POWER STATE EXERCISE

Begin by remembering a time in your life when you felt the exhilaration of accomplishment. Choose a high point. The time you won the fifty-yard dash . . . received an award . . . or received a hearty round of applause for a great speech. Recall an experience in which you felt totally confident. Try to recall what you were wearing, who was there, the exact setting, what you heard. Remember as many sensory details as you can. Allow yourself to remember how you felt so you can re-create this powerful feeling.

At the peak of this feeling, when you are breathing into this optimum emotional state, make a fist and say, "Yes."

Really hear the tone of voice you used when you were totally confident. Feel the way you held your body. See the way you looked. At the peak of this feeling, make a fist and once again declare, "Yes."

You are re-creating a feeling of strength and confidence. You are tapping into your sense memory of how it feels to succeed.

When you want to re-create this state, just make a fist and say, "Yes." This is your anchor to re-create your peak state.

Singing, Whistling, and Humming

My husband and I were paying our parking garage fee when he noticed that the attendant was singing. "You must be happy," he commented. "Not really," the attendant replied. We laughed because he was using singing to elevate his mood. This was something he did to alleviate stress. Singing, whistling, and humming all serve to soothe the nerves.

I have several clients who sing for inspiration. One woman, a pilot, has a workout room filled with mirrors. She puts on the *Chorus Line* album and orchestrates her own lyrics to "One singular sensation," changing the lyrics to "every little step I take . . ." She pumps her energy while dancing and singing into the mirror. Another woman uses the Whitney Houston version of "The Greatest Love of All" and belts out, "The greatest love of all is happening to me. I found the greatest love of all inside of me." This never fails to put her in a loving and compassionate mood. I know people who use everything from Disney's "Zip a Dee Doo Dah" to James Brown's "I Feel Good" to move their energy. Whether you sing in the shower, in your car, or in front of the mirror, sing and loosen up to your song. Let the music move you.

As your Star Quality develops, you experience this truth: Thought creates reality. You create your life through your thoughts, feelings, and actions. You may not be able to control the circumstances of the day, but you sure can control *your reaction* to them. You deserve to enjoy your life. As Lou Rawls sings, "It's supposed to be fun."

Accept that you have the power to change your life and that you can create the life you want. Use your energy to overpower your mind when it wanders into the negativity of troubles and trials. I've always felt that's what Jesus Christ meant when he said, "I have overcome the world." He overcame the negative thought that pulls us down.

You have choices. Your life is determined by the choices you make. In each situation, you can change your reaction. You cannot change others, but you can change yourself.

Stop Negative Patterns

Confront your negative patterns. Use your energy to defend against them. Don't be discouraged if you're working on something and you don't notice change immediately. Remember that it takes twenty-one days to change a habit.

I was in the habit of waking up in the morning and thinking of what I didn't like about my life. One morning, I was upset because a leg on a bronze statue I had purchased had been broken in shipping. I kept thinking about it until, suddenly, I started thinking about the other beautiful statues and art I enjoy. I felt the blessings of my life flood through me. It had taken some time, but I had broken the habit of morning fret and worry. I'd gotten myself back on track. Now, when I wake up and my mind wanders to problems, I shift to the big picture. I count my blessings. I appreciate what I have. I have beauty and love in my life *and* a bronze statue with a cracked leg.

If you're experiencing jealousy, anger, or fear, face it. When you feel stuck in a negative pattern, STOP. Remind yourself that you have a choice. You can choose to continue, or you can look for the lesson and see what it is you need to learn.

You lose power through fear. As a friend of mine says, "When the fear train rolls through my house, I don't get on it. I know where it's going!"

Self-power comes from your intention to use your energy for your highest good. You decide what's important to you and how you want to create your day. You decide just how much fulfillment and satisfaction you will let yourself experience. All the problems and challenges that meet you this day can either take you down or prod you to make better choices so that you change and grow.

Start your day by acknowledging that you have the power to change your life and to create the life you want. The secret here is:

You can only bring to life what you can imagine.

Use the power of your imagination to create possibilities for yourself. Once you understand that your mind creates your negative thoughts and attitudes, you can choose to use it to create *positive* ones. Instead of imagining yourself disappointed or unhappy, imagine yourself alive, loving, and happy.

Start your day with a visualization exercise.

MORNING VISUALIZATION EXERCISE

When you wake up, start your day with meditation, prayer, or a walk in nature. See your day flowing along. Imagine yourself strong and empowered, experiencing life with enthusiasm and good humor. Say out loud, "I control my thoughts and feelings. It's my intention to live a joyful Star Quality day. I accept the challenges that I encounter. Whatever life brings me today, I welcome it and know I am equal to it. I bring my energy, love, and power to this day."

Intention

When you have strengthened yourself, nothing can throw you off your rhythm. You may want to establish a new intention each day. Ask yourself, "What do I want to experience today?" Then answer the question. This is a good way to start your day.

Here are some possible intentions:

- to be passionate about what you do today
- to create a nourishing environment for yourself by choosing to spend time only with people who add to your life
- to lighten up and have fun
- to shower yourself with caring and love
- to present your ideas powerfully

Stay focused on the intention you set for today. You may not be responsible for all the day's events, but it's your reaction to these events that determines the quality of your life.

Accept what is given to you as exactly what is necessary for your growth. When the tests and the challenges come, stay detached and look for the lesson. *Everything is part of your growth.* This is how life teaches you.

Say this affirmation out loud with feeling: "I WANT WHAT I HAVE." Say it until you believe it and know it to be true. This acceptance will thrust you into the precious present moment that, as you know, is where happiness exists.

Naturalness and Humor

Star Quality people have two special characteristics. One is a *naturalness*, an ease that is very attractive. They have discovered that as fear goes, life flows. That gives them an *easy "up" energy* just like in the gospel song that goes: "This little light of mine, let it shine, let it shine." Star Quality people know how to let their light shine.

The second characteristic is a quality of *humor and playfulness* that allows them to make the best of a situation. I saw this illustrated recently when an obviously frazzled woman was late boarding a crowded airplane that was ready to take off for Mexico. She had two kids, and the younger one, a girl about two, got loose and started down the aisle squealing. Her mother let her go, faced a planeload full of people, and shouted, "Pick your seat mate, honey." Then, as her daughter went over and tried to grab a magazine out of some man's hand, she said, "It looks like you're the lucky one." Everyone laughed, and I marveled at the way she had turned a difficult situation into an enjoyable one.

A good laugh not only boosts your energy, it helps your body relax. Star Quality people know they've got nothing to defend, so they are free to be whoever they are. Because they have forgiven themselves and released their critical self-judgments, they have lightened up and are able to laugh at their experiences. They take their responsibility to themselves and to their lives seriously, but they take themselves lightly.

As someone brilliantly said, "Life is too important to be taken seriously." People should never take themselves so seriously that they can't laugh at themselves, the world, and the people in it. Star Quality shows itself in a playfulness, a lightness, a spontaneity; laughter erupts out of the sheer pleasure of living in this world.

There is an ease that develops from understanding that we are all evolving and that every event brings the possibility of furthering our growth. You stop seeing life as a chore in which you move heavily from one task to the next, and you start experiencing life as fun. It's our playfulness that allows us to experience the joy of life.

Children are naturally playful and fun-loving. As they grow into adults, they are not encouraged to keep this attitude. Commands like "Get serious" or "Knock it off" or "Wipe that silly smile off your face" are used to curtail our wild and playful sides. It didn't take much to get most of us to decide to avoid looking foolish. We have let the professional comedians tell the jokes. Too many of us have become part of the audience.

People who have developed their Star Quality participate in life. They take risks. They express their ideas, tell jokes. They're not even afraid to make fools of themselves. They realize that fun things happen when you get past being self-conscious. They have adopted an attitude of playfulness and have opened their minds to silly and outrageous thoughts.

There's always room for another laugh. Zen Buddhists have suggested starting the morning with fifteen minutes of laughter. They feel this will take care of the rest of the day. If you experience something funny, great, but if not, then fake laughter. Just start "ha ha ha-ing" and watch it roll into the real thing. Even fake laughter can start putting you in the frame of mind to enjoy your day.

Laughter has physiological benefits as well. Hearty laughter accelerates breathing and increases oxygen consumption. After laughing, your pulse rate and blood pressure drop and your muscles become more relaxed. The greater the intensity of your laughter, the more your body relaxes.

Not only is humor funny stuff, you can make more points with it than with anything else. Some people are naturally humorous. It's a blessing. If you don't think you're a funny person, then set an intention right now to change.

Jokes

In order to make a joke, you have to have a premise that something is wrong. You learn to make light of your complaints and your anxieties. When Jay Leno says, "You ever look at the expiration date on a bag of Wonder Bread? It says right there in tiny letters, 'Hey, pal, you should live so long.'" He's expressing his nutritional concerns with a humorous twist.

Humor needs to be used and cultivated. Rent videos of comedians performing. Go to comedy clubs and watch them perform live. Keep a joke book; write down jokes you find funny.

When you start working on joke delivery, here's what we suggest.

JOKE DELIVERY

1. Memorize the punch line first. It's the most important line of the joke, so practice it.
2. Memorize the rest of the joke.
3. Practice your joke out loud a few times.
4. Don't rush the delivery.
5. Deliver your joke to a friend first.
6. When you have it down, cut loose.

After you've built up your joke-telling skills, take risks and develop your own personal humorous style. Some of the best humor comes when we make fun of ourselves.

When you put enough distance between yourself and your experiences, you can enjoy their humor. Then you'll find it's safe to poke fun at yourself.

PEOPLE WHO FEED THE EARTH

People who have developed Star Quality have *worked on themselves*. They have become appreciative, caring people. I think of them as people who feed the earth. I was fascinated when I watched the movie *The Little Foxes* and heard Bette Davis (who plays Regina Giddens) described as one of the "people who eat the earth." It's such a powerful image. Think of people who eat the earth. They are self-centered, selfish, materialistic, have no sense of the needs of other people or of the needs of the planet on which they live. They manipulate to get what they want. They struggle for money and power so they can control circumstances to provide means for their own selfish ends.

I began to wonder: Who are the people who *feed* the earth? As I thought about this, I realized that, first of all, they must be people committed to loving *themselves*. They realize you can't help another person until you have helped yourself. So in order to feed the earth, you have to first feed yourself. Only when you take care of yourself are you able to take care of others. Smiles, helping hands, contributions, and service flow freely from someone who is full and giving from his overflow. Anger erupts out of those who have not fed themselves yet are trying to feed others.

A sure sign that you are learning to feed yourself is that you notice you are much better at choosing people. You begin to surround yourself with people who support your growth, people who nourish you, whose values you admire. People you can learn from and who teach you about life. You will notice that what is within you surrounds you, and you will be choosing to be with people who are like you—people who feed the earth.

STAR QUALITY STARS

The ability to be completely yourself ignites the Star Quality inside you. When you're relaxed and confident, you have no trouble expressing yourself by speaking from your heart. You're not thinking about how you look or sound. You know you look and sound just fine. You're not thinking about what anyone else thinks of you. You know who you are.

You give yourself the love and admiration that adds up to Star Treatment because you understand that nothing outside you can make you whole.

Stars create themselves by doing the work that is required to free themselves up to play the starring role in their lives. They understand that actors are paid to play characters. Stars always play themselves.

Continue increasing your self-power. Work with the exercises. Master the Seven Points of Star Quality.

Stars are made, not born.
Nervousness is normal, so *use* it.
You can *tell* your feelings how to feel.
You're only as big as you think you are.
Words can either wound or heal.
True power comes from within.
You deserve Star Treatment.

Keep going. Keep improving. Do the work. Clear out stuck beliefs. Let go of fear. Strengthen your walks and talks. Love yourself. Center yourself.

You can get help with anything. You can heal the pain and the fear in your mind and heart. No emotional, physical, or mental block can stop you unless you decide it can.

You are unique and have something of value to contribute to the world. By now, you know that the applause, the love, the admiration come from inside you. You own your power. You celebrate life. You are a precious being, a Star Quality star.

ACKNOWLEDGMENTS

I am grateful to my mother and father for the lessons they taught me and the ways they helped me grow. Certain people who offered me a bigger picture, comforting words, and a belief in better possibilities also stand out. They are my Grannie Pyle; my fifth-grade teacher, Mrs. Ackerman; and my college psychology professor, Dr. Fisher.

Spiritual teachers, like Brugh Joy, held a light for me and helped my own to burn brighter. Seers and astrologers were helpful in pointing out to me the places where I had stuck patterns so that I could heal myself and continue to grow, particularly Vedic astrologer Chakrapani Udall. Remarkable friends pushed, supported, and challenged me; my sister, Leigh, and especially Elisa Lodge, who first enlivened me with the concept of Star Quality.

My very best friend, my husband, Orson, carries so much of what is strong, whole, and knowing and exemplifies masculinity for me. My son, Zack, never stops showing me his courage and his sensitivity in his quest for true power. My daughter, Zoe, is learning to trust life and to play in it.

My literary agent, Ed Victor, was strong and sure as he saw this book and pushed me to get it on paper. My publisher, Clare Ferraro, with her gentle sensitivity, understood the promise of *Star Quality*. My editor, Peter Gethers, was both clear and strong as he directed me to shape and focus *Star Quality*. . . . And Tom Alderman and Carey Grange continually gave me the best On Camera support.

I thank Mother and Father God for guiding me and for showing me my way. All of these people have helped me to follow the star inside of me, shown me the light that each of us carries, and made me certain that each one of us has the ability to shine.

INDEX

Acting as if, 108–9
Addictions, 62–63
Affirmations
  and negative beliefs, 100–5
  self-supportive, 112–15
  top ten, 105
Anger
  handling of, 68–72, 214–15
  and sadness, 69, 72–73
Appearance, acceptance of, 92–96, 120–23
Autosuggestion, to change beliefs, 100–2

Beliefs
  and affirmations, 102–5
  and autosuggestion, 100–1
  distorted, letting go of, 96–99
  power of, 95–96, 97–98
Breathing
  diaphragmatic, 47–48
  rhythmic, 48
Business meetings
  visualization for, 55

Cathartic relaxation, 241
Centering, 222
Clothing
  choosing, 172–73
  color of, 173–74
Communication skills. See
  Public speaking; Talk
Complaining, 194–95
Crying, 72–73

Dark side, 218–19
Detachment, 219–21
Diaphragmatic breathing, 47–48
Diet, 242–43

Empathy, 83
Energy
  channeling of, 49
  and feelings, 61
Energy boosters, 243–51
  energy pumping, 246–47

exercise, 244–45
  humor, 252–55
  massage therapy, 245–46
  singing/humming/whistling, 248–49
  visualization, 250–51
Enthusiasm, power of, 246
Exercise, 244–45
Eye contact, 142–47
  blinking, 146
  negative contact, 146–47
  power eye gestures, 143–44
  power of, 143, 144

Facial expressions, 139–42
  and feelings, 141
  smiling, 141–42
Fear, 37–40
  embracing of, 39
  and growth, 37–38
  letting go of, 219–20
  perpetuating, 51
  releasing fear exercise, 40
Feeders of Earth, 255–56
Feelings, 8
  and addictions, 62–63
  anger, 68–72
  as contagious, 79–80
  control of, 61–62
  emotional healing, 64–69
  as energy source, 61
  and facial expressions, 141
  and thoughts, 84–90
Feeling talk, 179–81
First impressions, 42–43, 150–51
Forgiveness, of self, 73–79
Frustration, 40–41

Generosity, 229
Gestures, 133–39
  distracting, 134–35
  guidelines for, 135–37
  negative, 135
  of power, 137–39
God force, 220–21
Growth, versus homeostasis, 19–20

Health
  diet, 242–43
  energy boosters, 243–51
  and stress, 240–42
Humming, 248–49
Humor, 252–55
  benefits of, 252–54
  jokes, 254–55

Imperfection, acceptance of, 91–93,
    234–35
Intentions, 251–52
Interviews, visualization for, 57
Intuition, and trust, 215–16, 217–18

Jokes, 254–55

Listening, 204–6
Love
  and healing, 81
  self-love, 80–83

Massage therapy, 245–46
Meditation, 225–26
Mental rehearsal, 51–52
Mindfulness, 222–23
Mistakes, learning from, 90
Monotone voice, 165–67
Mumbling, 158–59
Muscle tension, releasing, 45–46

Nasal voice, 159–60
Naturalness, 252
Nature, 226–27
Neck relaxation, 245
Negativity, changing
  acting as if, 108–10
  with affirmations, 100–5, 112–15
  with autosuggestion, 100–2
  confronting negative patterns, 249–50
  with pep talks, 110–12
  with thoughts, 107–8
  time frame for, 102
Nervousness, 7, 27–57
  and fear, 37–40
  positive use of, 28, 33–34, 35
  and public speaking, 29–31, 35–36
  and shyness, 41–43
  signs of, 28, 34–35
Nervousness management, 44–57
  relaxation, 44–49
  visualization, 33, 50–57
Nervous speech, 157–58
Nonverbal communication
  eye contact, 142–47
  facial expressions, 139–42

gestures, 133–39
  meeting for first time, 150
  physical presence, 124–33
  rapport, 168–74
  reading people, 132–33
  touch, 147–50
  voice, 151–68

On Camera, 11–13
Oneness experience, 220–21

Personal space, 149–50
Physical presence, 124–33
  posture, 124–26
  walk, 126–31
Posture, 124–26
  body alignment exercise, 125–26
  body energizer exercise, 126
Power
  and centering, 223, 224
  and detachment, 219–21
  generosity of spirit, 229
  inner radiance, 228
  inner strength, 228–30
  source of, 210
  and spiritual practice, 224–27
  and staying present, 221–23
  and trust, 212–19
Prayer, power of, 224
Presence walk, 128–29
Present, staying in, 221–23
Public presentations
  visualization for, 56
Public speaking, 199–204
  answering questions, 202–3
  and nervousness, 29–31, 35–36
  one-on-one method, 36
  talking from the heart, 199–202

Rapport, 168–74
  conversational rhythm, 171–72
  and likability, 169
  mirroring of another, 169–70
  and personal appearance, 172–73
Relaxation, 44–49
  breathing, 46–48
  channeling energy exercise, 49
  muscle tension release, 46
Rhythmic breathing, 48

Sadness, and anger, 69, 72–73
Self, listening to, 105–8
Self-acceptance, 17–19, 62, 87
  acceptance exercise, 76
  of imperfection, 91–93, 234–35
  and inner beliefs, 96–99

modeling of, 93–96
  of physical self, 92–96, 120–23
  self-forgiveness, 73–79
Self-criticism, 87–90, 107
Self-discipline, 62
Self-esteem, "acting as if," 108–9
Self-forgiveness, 76–79
Self-love, 14, 80–83, 233–34
Self-talk
  for negative beliefs, 86–90
  pep talk exercise, 110–12
  self-supportive affirmations, 112–15
Self-worth, 234–37
Shyness, 41–43
Singing, 248–49
Smiling, 141–42
Social settings, visualization for, 54
Spiritual practice, 224–27
  meditation, 225–26
  nature as, 226–27
  prayer, 224
  Sabbath observance, 227
Spontaneous talk, 178–79
Star Quality
  meaning of, 5–6, 16
  Seven Points of Power, 7–8, 256
  sustaining of, 210–11
Star Quality Quiz, 22–24
Steeple gesture, 138–39
Stress, 240–41
  scanning body for, 241
Stress management, 241–42
  cathartic relaxation, 241
  neck-relaxation exercise, 245
  therapeutic relaxation, 241

Talk
  complaining, 194–95
  feeling talk, 179–81
  hedging/qualifying, 192–93
  nonwords, 193–94
  should/trying in, 192
  spontaneous talk, 178–79
  truth talk, 181–83
Talk tactics
  alignment techniques, 184–85
  and delicate issues, 189–90
  interruption techniques, 190–91

"I" versus "You" messages, 191–92
  positive language, 185–87
  power talk, 195–204
  public speaking, 199–204
  for selling, 196–97
  tailoring speech to person, 198–99
  undertalking, 187–88
Therapeutic relaxation, 241
Therapy, process of, 64–69
Thoughts, and feelings, 84–90
Touch, 147–50
  personal space, 149–50
  practicing use of, 148–49
Trust, 212–19
  and facing dark side, 217–19
  and intuition, 215–16, 217–18

Victim, self as, 67, 217
Visualization, 50–57
  for business meetings, 55
  of fear fantasies, 51
  for interviews, 57
  mental rehearsal, 51–52
  nervousness management, 33
  for public presentations, 56
  for social settings, 54
  to start day, 250–51
  steps in, 52
Voice, 10, 151–68
  common defects, 153
  fast/slow talkers, 155–56
  inflecting up at end of sentence, 162–63
  interruptions, 154
  loud/soft talkers, 163–65
  monotone, 165–67
  mumbling, 158–59
  nasality, 159–60
  nervous, gasping, 157–58
  shrillness, 160–62
  throat comfort tips, 154
  voice power tips, 167–68

Walk
  power walk, 129–30
  presence walk, 128–29
Whistling, 248–49
Work/career, 237–39
Worrying, 43–44

About the Author

Christen Brown is the founder of ON CAMERA, a Los Angeles–based company that has prepared authors, athletes, and average, everyday people for media appearances.